T0330948

ROUTLEDGE LIBRARY EDITIONS: INTERNATIONAL SECURITY STUDIES

Volume 1

ALTERNATIVE DEFENCE POLICY

ALTERNATIVE DEFENCE POLICY

Edited by
GORDON BURT

Routledge
Taylor & Francis Group

LONDON AND NEW YORK

First published in 1988 by Croom Helm Ltd

This edition first published in 2021
by Routledge
2 Park Square, Milton Park, Abingdon, Oxon OX14 4RN

and by Routledge
52 Vanderbilt Avenue, New York, NY 10017

Routledge is an imprint of the Taylor & Francis Group, an informa business

British Library Cataloguing in Publication Data
A catalogue record for this book is available from the British Library

ISBN: 978-0-367-68499-0 (Set)
ISBN: 978-1-00-316169-1 (Set) (ebk)
ISBN: 978-0-367-71044-6 (Volume 1) (hbk)
ISBN: 978-0-367-71046-0 (Volume 1) (pbk)
ISBN: 978-1-00-314906-4 (Volume 1) (ebk)

Publisher's Note
The publisher has gone to great lengths to ensure the quality of this reprint but
points out that some imperfections in the original copies may be apparent.

Disclaimer
The publisher has made every effort to trace copyright holders and would welcome
correspondence from those they have been unable to trace.

ALTERNATIVE DEFENCE POLICY

Edited by
GORDON BURT

CROOM HELM
London • New York • Sydney

© 1988 Gordon Burt
Croom Helm Ltd, Provident House, Burrell Row,
Beckenham, Kent, BR3 1AT
Croom Helm Australia, 44-50 Waterloo Road,
North Ryde, 2113, New South Wales

Published in the USA by
Croom Helm
in association with Methuen, Inc.
29 West 35th Street
New York, NY 10001

British Library Cataloguing in Publication Data

Alternative defence policy.
   1.Great Britain — Military policy
   I. Burt, Gordon
   355'.0335'41   UA647
   0-7099-5038-1

Library of Congress Cataloging in Publication Data

0-7099-5038-1

Printed and bound in Great Britain by
Biddles Ltd, Guildford and King's Lynn

CONTENTS

CONTRIBUTORS

Gordon Burt, Institute of Educational Technology, The Open University

Andrew Kelly, School of Peace Studies, University of Bradford

Philip Gummett, Department of Science and Technology Policy, Manchester University

Mike Gapes, Research Officer, Policy Development Directorate, The Labour Party

Patrick Dunleavy, Politics Department, London School of Economics and Political Science

FOREWORD

The main chapters in this book are based on papers prepared for a conference on Alternative Defence Policy organised by the Conflict Research Society. The papers have been revised in the light of discussion at the conference and subsequent exchanges between the authors. To these chapters have been added by introduction and conclusion.

The final stages of the preparation of this book have witnessed events which give urgency to many of the arguments presented here. We hope that this book will provide a useful contribution to the intensifying debates, firstly about the future direction of British defence policy - and secondly about the political strategies which are needed, if we are to bring about changes in Britain's existing defence policy.

ACKNOWLEDGEMENT

We gratefully acknowledge permission from Gallup and MORI to reproduce findings from their opinion polls in Table 5.1 on page 112.

Chapter One

INTRODUCTION TO THE CRISIS

Gordon Burt

The ballot papers of just forty-two per cent of British voters on 11th June 1987 should not be taken as the final judgment on present NATO policy. For the correct analysis of the situation remains the same:

> There is now less and less likelihood that the West would authorise the use of any nuclear weapons except in response to a Soviet nuclear attack. There is, therefore, slow but discernible movement toward acceptance of three facts: the West's existing plans for initiating the use of nuclear weapons, if ever implemented, are far more likely to destroy Western Europe, the United States and Japan than to defend them; whatever deterrent value remains in our nuclear strategy is eroding; the strength, and hence the deterrent capability, of Western conventional forces can be increased substantially within realistic political and financial constraints.

Yet most voters are unaware of these facts:

> Most Americans and Europeans are unaware that Western strategy now calls for early initiation of the use of nuclear weapons in a conflict with the Soviet Union. Polls indicate that 80% of Americans believe we wouldn't use such weapons unless the Soviets fired them first. They would be shocked to learn they're mistaken. And they'd be horrified to know that senior military commanders believe that to carry out our present strategy would lead to destruction of our society. But

1

those are the facts.

In truth, the emperor has no clothes. Our current nuclear strategy is indeed bankrupt. (Robert McNamara, Guardian, 29th June 1987).

British defence policy in particular is in a state of crisis. It is under siege from critics of all persuasions and at all levels of society. (1) Although it is the peace movement which mounts the most radical and the most sustained critique of present policy, this merely represents the tip of the iceberg. The Labour party and certain sections of the Alliance parties all have policies requiring a radical change in the current defence policy. (2) And even within the Conservative party we have pressure groups like 'Tories Against Cruise and Trident', and radical alternatives such as that offered by Peter Johnson. (3) Nor does present policy find unanimous endorsement from the military. For we can point to such high-level 'dissidents' as Earl Mountbatten and Lord Carver, as well as to popular involvement in Ex-Servicemen's CND. (4)

Nor should we restrict ourselves to a purely insular perspective. For the British crisis is in part a reflection of the much wider crises in NATO policy as a whole. (5) It coincides with crises in other US alliances such as ANZUS. And at its most fundamental it reflects the crisis in world security overall. In response to this crisis, the international character of the peace movement is well illustrated by such European-wide organisations as END, by well-established US-Europe links such as that relating to the Nuclear Freeze Campaign, by various East-West links such as East-West Reach, and by links with peace movements in the Southern hemisphere. (6) Here again the global peace movement merely represents the tip of the iceberg. In Western Europe, we find many major political parties and some governments challenging the assumptions of NATO policy. In the United States we find such major political figures as Edward Kennedy, Robert McNamara, McGeorge Bundy and George Kennan challenging US defence policy. (7) To an even greater extent than their British counterparts, the US military have given birth to several prominent 'dissidents'. In addition the United States has experienced problems with allies such as Greece. Even in the Warsaw Pact countries we can find challenges to the existing system of confrontation. Not only are there the dissident and suppressed peace groups, but we can also point to the involvement of Soviet scientists in the debate with Western scientists about the nuclear winter. (8) The Rumanian government and the Soviet Peace Committee are perhaps the mirror-opposites of official or highly-placed voices in the West which criticise the existing military system without straying too far from 'acceptable' opinion. (9) Finally and importantly we should not ignore the persistent criticism of the superpower arms race by the countries of the Third World. Though their voices can be heard but faintly, the starving children of the sub-Saharan countries are critics too.

But let us return to insularity. What is the nature of the crisis in British defence policy? It has, I think, two basic components. The first component is indicated in the previous paragraph: the British crisis is partly a reflection of global crisis. The second component is peculiar to Britain - what we are seeing is 'merely' the most recent manifestation of Britain's century-long decline from world hegemony to middle-ranking power. Even if we accept the global military system (which I do not), this fact alone would demand a radical change to Britain's defence policy (see Johnson).

Let us start by considering the global crisis. Here again we should distinguish two aspects. In one sense what we are witnessing is something very familiar to the historian of world politics: we are witnessing radical changes in the distribution of world power, and we are experiencing the crises which invariably accompany such radical changes. (10) In order to appreciate what these radical changes are, it is helpful to look back to the transformation of global power brought about by the Second World War. Before that war, the world military system was dominated by several 'great powers', with Britain possessing a waning hegemony. (11) Most of these powers were dissipated as a result of their war efforts, and Britain's hegemony ceased. What was left was the overwhelming military superiority of the two superpowers, with the United States taking over Britain's role of world hegemony. The subsequent history of the world has been substantially influenced by this US hegemony and the related superpower confrontation. This period has also seen a slow but continuous erosion of this structure. Slowly we have seen:

-   the gradual replacement of US monopoly or superiority in the military sphere, by an 'order of magnitude' parity between the superpowers;

- the gradual recovery of Western Europe and Eastern Europe relative to their respective superpowers ... both in economic and in military terms, and (to a varying degree) in terms of political independence; (12)
- the not-so-gradual recovery of Japan, first in the economic sphere, and, more recently, in terms of a resurgence of militarism, and the adoption of a more active military role (carefully fostered by the USA); (13)
- the emergence of China as a fledgling superpower;
- more gradually, the emergence in the Third World of certain countries as major regional powers, against a background of greater political (if not economic) independence in the Third World.

In part, then, our present crisis consists of challenges to the two superpowers from lesser powers, as the latter become aware of their increasing independence (relatively speaking). In response, we observe the frantic and often tragic attempts by the superpowers to reassert their authority.

The transition from hegemony to plurality has occurred many times before in world history. This time, however, things are different. We now have nuclear weapons. It is this which presents the second distinctive aspect of the crisis. For now the fundamental contradiction of militarism is clear to everyone. By our 'defence' we shall destroy ourselves and the world as well.

These are not just dramatic statements. The post-war world has seen a more-or-less continual increase in the number, the destructiveness and the 'sophistication' of nuclear weapons systems. The potential effects of any nuclear war have grown correspondingly more horrendous. Scientific research has indicated how yesterday's fears are much too optimistic: the prospect of nuclear winter has made the hawks less happy in their bunkers. (14)

'Of course, the whole point of deterrence is that it prevents all this happening!' Here again, scientific assessment casts increasing doubt on this cosy assumption. First, military and government officials don't believe it: they attach significant probabilities to the event of a nuclear war. Moreover, the nature of the command and control systems in the two blocs suggests that the outbreak of a serious crisis is quite likely to trigger an accidental nuclear war, due to the failure to identify a false alarm correctly. (15)

The nature of the crisis is that our security relies on a dangerous superstition.

However, there are absurdities within absurdities. Absurd as the super-power confrontation is, we can look within it and find other more specific absurdities. One such is our present NATO defence policy. It would appear to have been purpose-built so that a small, local, conventional incident rapidly and uncontrollably escalates into all-out nuclear war.

Let us now consider that aspect of the crisis which is peculiar to Britain. As noted earlier this relates to the fact that Britain has experienced a steady decline in relative power. Texts on the post-war history of British foreign policy all subscribe to this as the dominant theme, e.g. Northedge's 'The descent from power'. (16) Moreover, as well as stressing the reduction in Britain's power as a consequence of the war, they also identify a much longer-term process of decline - as exemplified by the fact that Britain's rate of economic growth was overtaken by countries such as Germany and the United States in the nineteenth century. This lower level of economic growth has persisted right through to the present day. As Britain's economic power has dwindled, it has step by step relinquished central roles in the world economy. (17)

In turn this reduced economic base has necessitated a reduced global role for Britain - with the liberation of peoples from colonisation, and the reduction in overseas military commitments. In retrospect, what has been so surprising has been the controversiality of the obvious and the inevitable. Repeatedly there have been attempts to hang on to traditional roles - and even to attempt to regain roles which had been lost - despite the fact that Britain lacks the power to fulfill these roles. The experience in the Falklands indicates how costly this can be.

Our possession of an independent nuclear deterrent is another such anachronism. From its inception, it was seen as a ticket to 'a seat at the top table'. Now that Britain has so clearly not got a seat at the top table, the possession of nuclear weapons would need to be justified in terms of providing national security. However, no-one has ever managed to provide a plausible scenario for the usefulness of Britain's independent deterrent. Not only is the independent deterrent militarily useless, it is also expensive. The money would be better spent on conventional defence, or on constructive foreign policy, or on rebuilding the devastated communities of Britain. However, scrapping our nuclear deterrent would simply leave Britain as an active member in a nuclear alliance, with nuclear forces occupying British territory and with British forces still linked into the nuclear force structure in NATO. As I have indicated earlier, these nuclear forces are embedded in a NATO strategy which is fundamentally flawed. It is the purpose of this book to formulate and analyse an alternative defence policy which overcomes these defects.

Now there are a number of fundamental dilemmas which face any defence policy. The first of these has been referred to as the 'security dilemma'. (18) Too lax a defence runs the risk of ignoring enemies. Too belligerent a defence runs the risk of creating enemies. The latter danger is relevant to our present policy: threatening the total devastation of a country would appear to be an extremely effective method of creating enemies. In order to remedy this, we are led to examine 'non-provocative' defence policies. However, we must also avoid the risk of ignoring enemies. How can we discover who our enemies are? Theory suggests several criteria:

(i)   we should fear large, military powerful countries;
(ii)   we should fear countries close at hand (i.e. geopolitically close) more than distant countries;
(iii)   we should fear countries which have in the past intervened in other countries' affairs;
(iv)   we should fear countries which adopt belligerent rhetoric against countries which fail to conform to the 'true' ideology;
(v)   we should fear countries which have a motive for intervention;
(vi)   we should fear countries which are unstable ... and those which are stable?;
(vii)   we should fear countries which already have a foothold in our own country;
(viii) we should fear countries hostile towards us;
(ix)   we would fear countries whose defence policies are directed against us.

The interesting point about these criteria is that they don't provide a decisive distinction between the Soviet Union on the one hand and the United States or even France on the other. Certainly the USSR is geopolitically closer than the USA. However, only the last two criteria manage to single out the Soviet Union alone. Yet these two criteria carry a flavour of self-fulfilling prophecy and circular reasoning: the Soviet Union is our enemy because the Soviet Union is our enemy! (19)

Now that we know who our enemy is, we can get down to business! What exactly is our enemy threatening? Firstly, even conservative assessments acknowledge that there is no immediate intention on the Soviet Union's part to cross the border into Western Europe. However, what does seem to underlie Western policy is the feeling that under certain circumstances (which are seldom clearly specified) in the future, unless the West has adequate defences, then an attack is to be expected. From hereon we assume that this is the central threat to Britain's security.

The dominant response in the face of such a threat is to establish a defence against the threat. And it is this kind of response which we shall be focussing on in this book. In the chapter which follows, Andrew Kelly will be asking what is 'the most appropriate form of defence for Western Europe against a threat from Eastern Europe'? The main thrust of his argument is that present NATO strategy is dangerous and unnecessary: dangerous in that it presents a low threshold for an escalation to nuclear war, and unnecessary in that it is based on the questionable assumption that NATO's conventional forces would be over-run in any Warsaw Pact attack. To demonstrate the falsity of the assumption, Kelly considers the numerical balances for different military categories, and identifies non-numerical aspects which modify these balances (e.g. equipment reliability). Using this analysis, he then considers a variety of scenarios and concludes that NATO can withstand the attack using only its conventional forces. He then goes on to suggest how NATO's present conventional forces can be modified in order to improve conventional deterrence. This is done by strengthening defences, e.g. through the use of physical barriers, and by adopting non-provocative strategies.

An alternative strategy for conventional deterrence is the Follow-on Forces Attack strategy, in association with the new conventional technology. However, Philip Gummett casts serious doubts on the wisdom of such a strategy. In contrast to the optimistic claims which are often made for the new technology, he points out that this technology is still at a very early stage of development and we can be certain neither about the costs nor about the performance.

In operations, the new technology could well be vulnerable to countermeasures. Furthermore, at the strategic level, it suffers severe drawbacks. For its deep-strike capability encourages pre-emption, while the 'virtue' of force multiplication presents a force which is less visible and hence possibly less of a deterrent. Finally it blurs the distinction between conventional and nuclear, thus increasing the danger of an escalation to the use of nuclear weapons, and posing verification problems for arms control agreements.

Thus far the discussion has focussed on the military dimension. However, it is important to emphasise the diversity of political issues which touch on our central concern for defence policy. For discussions of defence policy quickly lead into discussions of foreign policy, budgetary policy and domestic politics. This suggests that an alternative defence policy, in addition to making strategic sense, must also be capable of being implemented in a particular political context. Mike Gapes provides an interesting account of how the Labour Party's non-nuclear defence policy has matured in parallel with a changing political context, and considers how the national and international political context which might prevail at the next general election could affect the chances of implementing that policy.

The following chapter examines the problem which is crucial for the implementation of this policy: how might a non-militarist British Government be elected? Here Patrick Dunleavy identifies a key dilemma. For an electoral promise to create a non-nuclear Britain would not presently find favour amongst the voting public. On the other hand, the continuation of present policy is too dangerous. Hence Dunleavy suggests that the public should be given the opportunity to debate the issue, and the power to decide the issue by means of a referendum. His arguments rest on an interesting analysis of public attitudes to various defence issues. In addition he makes the important point that public opinion is dynamic - it changes - but that it seldom changes very quickly. Hence his conclusion that a future government should foster the growth and development of opinion on this issue, rather than rule by diktat.

In reviewing these contributions, a clear picture emerges. In this picture we can see quite clearly the flawed nature of current defence policy. Its flaws can be found at different political levels: at the level of the superpower confrontation itself, at the level of NATO strategy, at the level of Britain's role in NATO, and even at the level of British domestic politics. On the positive side, the authors offer various alternatives for each of these levels: specifically a non-provocative conventional strategy for NATO, a process for changing NATO from within, a process for changing the super-power confrontation, and a process for democratic debate within Britain on these issues. Only when this programme has been accomplished, will Britain have escaped from its present crisis.

NOTES AND REFERENCES

1.   Tucker, R.W. The nuclear debate. Foreign Affairs 63, 1, 1-32, 1984.
2.   Defence and security for Britain. Labour Party, 1984. Healey, D. Labour and a world society. Fabian Tract 501, 1985. Defence and disarmament in Europe: policy document No. 5. Social Democratic Party, 1983.
3.   Johnson, P. Neutrality: a policy for Britain. Temple Smith, 1985.
4.   Mountbatten, Speech on the occasion of the award of the Louise Weiss Foundation Prize to SIPRI at Strasbourg on 11 May 1979. Field Marshall Lord Carver. A policy for peace. Faber and Faber, 1982.
5.   Pierre, A.J. The conventional defense of Europe: new technologies and new strategies. Council on Foreign Relations, New York, 1986.
6.   Yankelovich, D. and Doble, T. The public mood: nuclear weapons and the USSR. Foreign Affairs 63, 1, 33-46, 1984. Van Voorst, L.B. The churches and nuclear deterrence. Foreign Affairs 61, 4, 827-52, 1983.
7.   McGeorge Bundy, George F. Kennan, Robert S. McNamara and Gerard Smith. Nuclear Weapons and the Atlantic Alliance. Foreign Affairs 60, 4, 753-68, 1982.
      McNamara, R.S. The military role of nuclear weapons: perceptions and misperceptions. Foreign Affairs 62, 1, 59-80 1983.
      McGeorge Bundy, George F. Kennan, Robert S. McNamara and Gerard Smith. The President's choice: star wars or arms control. Foreign Affairs 63, 2, 264-78, 1984.
8.   Sakharov, A. The danger of thermo-nuclear war. Foreign Affairs 61, 5, 1001-61, 1983.
9.   Inozemtsev, N. Peace and Disarmament Academic

Studies. Progress Publishers, Moscow, 1980.

10.   There has been renewed academic interest in the rise-and-fall of hegemonies: Gilpin, R. War and change in world politics. Cambridge, USA, 1981. Modelski, G. Global wars and world leadership selection. Second World Congress of Arts and Sciences, Rotterdam, 1984.

11.   Northedge, F.S. The Troubled Giant: Britain among the Great Powers, 1916-1939. Bell, 1966.

12.   Brzezinski, Z. The future of Yalta. Foreign Affairs 63, 2, 279-302, 1984 ... and also other contributions in that issue on Europe by Richard Lowenthal, Walther Kiep, and Geoffrey Howe.

Bull, H. European self-reliance and the reform of NATO. Foreign Affairs 61, 4, 874-92, 1982.

Cohen, E.A. The long-term crisis of the alliance. Foreign Affairs 61, 2, 325-43, 1982.

13.   'Future historians may well mark the mid-1980s as the time when Japan surpassed the United States to become the world's dominant economic power'. Vogel, E.F. Pax Nipponica? Foreign Affairs 64, 4, 752-67, 1986.

14.   Sagan, C. Nuclear war and climatic catastrophe: some policy implications. Foreign Affairs 62, 1, 257-92, 1983.

15.   Bracken, P. The command and control of nuclear forces. Yale University Press, 1983.

Babst, D.U., Dely, A., Krieger, D. and Aldridge, R.C. Accidental nuclear war: the growing peril. Peace Research Institute, Dundas, Ontario, 1984.

Wallace, M.D. Accidental nuclear war: a risk assessment. Second World Congress of Arts and Sciences, Rotterdam, 1984.

16.   Northedge, F.S. Descent from power. British Foreign Policy, 1945-1973. Allen and Unwin, 1974.

Frankel, J. British Foreign Policy, 1945-1973. Oxford, 1975.

Jones, R.E. The changing structure of British Foreign Policy. Longman, 1974.

17.   Porter, B. Britain, Europe and the World 1850-1982: Delusions of Grandeur. Allen and Unwin, 1983.

18.   See the respective discussions of the security dilemma and of the 'prisoners' dilemma' in: Buzan, B. People, states and fear. Wheatsheaf, 1983. Baugh, W.H. The politics of nuclear balance. Longman, 1984.

19.   Smith applies Jervis' general arguments about misperception to the particular case of Western perceptions

of the Soviet Union. Smith, S. The myth of the Soviet threat. <u>RUSI</u> 127, 2, 41-49, 1982. Jervis, R. <u>Perception and misperception in international politics.</u> Princeton University Press, 1976.

Chapter Two

THE CONVENTIONAL BALANCE AND CONVENTIONAL DETERRENCE IN EUROPE

Andrew Kelly

INTRODUCTION

For the past thirty-five years NATO's basic strategy for responding to an invasion by the Warsaw Pact (WP) has been the threat of nuclear retaliation. This strategy of flexible response envisaged that the West would respond with nuclear weapons if a Soviet conventional attack succeeded in breaking through NATO's defences. It was argued that the West could not afford to match the Pact's conventional forces on economic grounds and that, consequently, the major factor in NATO's defence was the possession of a nuclear force.

In recent years, however, increasing attention has been devoted to the conventional component of the West's defence. The adoption by NATO of the concept of Follow on Forces Attack (FOFA) in November 1984 and the role of the Airland Battle doctrine in the US Army (together with the development and acquisition of new conventional technologies) are claimed as representing major steps forward in this process. In addition to these, a number of reports and proposals from groups as diverse as the Union of Concerned Scientists (UCS), (1) the British Atlantic Committee, (2) the European Security Study, (3) and the Alternative Defence Commission (ADC) (4) have concluded that an increased reliance on the use of conventional forces is the most favourable way forward. Within such proposals (including FOFA and Airland Battle) however, there are major differences, particularly concerning the role of nuclear weapons and the nature, and extent, of offensive strategies towards the WP. Whilst, for example, the FOFA

12

concept envisages attacks up to the three Westernmost military districts of the USSR (and includes the maintenance of NATO's nuclear forces) the more radical position outlined by the ADC sees a move towards a strategy of non-provocative, defensive deterrence with a significant de-emphasis of the nuclear role.

The intention of this paper is to examine the possibilities of moving towards conventional deterrence in Europe. Before the examination of FOFA, Airland Battle and defensive deterrence, however, it is necessary to examine two contingent factors: firstly, what should be the goals in transforming NATO strategy and, secondly, the military balance of conventional forces in Europe. Much of the analysis which follows is devoted to the balance in the central front area, although related factors (such as the air and naval balance) are considered. This is not to deny the importance of the flanks and other areas; rather the central front is where most public attention has been devoted.

TRANSFORMING NATO

A detailed examination of the military situation in Europe would confirm that fundamental change is necessary. The sheer size of the West's nuclear forces, and the real problems of controlling such forces in a crisis, together with the current policy of early nuclear first use, highlight the need to move away from a nuclear-based defence. Correspondingly, it is also clear that much more could be done in bolstering conventional defence on the central front.

Any change in NATO strategy, therefore, should have three main objectives: firstly, it should ensure that conventional deterrence is strengthened and that confidence is high that the Pact could not engage in a successful invasion of the West; secondly, that this change significantly raises the nuclear threshold for both sides (it should commence, for example, with the declaration of a policy of no-first-use of nuclear weapons and have, as a primary aim, the removal of nuclear weapons altogether from NATO's European strategy); and, thirdly, that the costs involved in such a transition should not be prohibitive. As a longer-term objective, any shift in NATO's strategy should be aimed at making a major contribution to curbing the nuclear arms race and reducing tension between the superpowers. It will be against these objectives that the current proposals and

13

new concepts will be examined.

THE BALANCE OF FORCES: NATO AND THE WARSAW PACT

The traditional view of the balance of conventional forces in Europe is that of a situation of overwhelming superiority in favour of the WP. However, whilst such a position may have been correct in the past, (and there is considerable evidence that doubts even this claim (5)) it is difficult to argue the case now. Over the past few years a number of accounts of the conventional balance have appeared which indicate that, whilst the Pact may continue to possess a crude <u>numerical</u> superiority, when related factors are fully taken into account there results a more favourable position for the West. (6)

There have always been major problems with assessing Soviet capabilities, not least in that the Soviet Union itself refuses to publish more than the bare minimum of information on its own armed forces. However, the traditional restriction to a straight numerical equation - the 'bean count' - has considerable limitations. As Mearsheimer has argued, success in a future conflict will be '... a function of strategy, not of overwhelming numbers.' (7) Thus, in an overall assessment of the potential Soviet threat to the West, it is necessary to examine, <u>inter alia,</u> intentions as well as capabilities, operational differences between the two forces, the advantages of the defence over the offence, the size and availability of reinforcements, the geography of the region, and the reliability of allies.

General Comparisons between NATO and the Warsaw Pact

Before moving on to the detailed discussion of the conventional balance, it is instructive to briefly survey the general economic, military and demographic factors of the two Alliances. Figure 2.1 provides this overview for the whole of NATO and the WP. Figure 2.2 provides the same information for the United States (US) and the Soviet Union (SU). From this it is possible to draw the conclusion that the West generally holds the advantage. Even where the SU possesses an advantage over the US (as it does in some of the major categories), this is more than equalled when the

Western European countries are included in the totals. Take, for example, the three categories of military expenditure, population and gross national product. Between the two Alliances the differences are stark. In 1983 NATO outspent the WP (in constant 1982 dollars) by $24.3 billion; had a population advantage of 208.2 million people and had a gross national product (in constant 1982 dollars) of well over double that of the WP.

A further indication of the strength of the West over the WP is contained in the annual report from the US Undersecretary of Defense for Research and Engineering. Here, in a comparison (in 1986) between the SU and the US of 20 key basic military technologies, he found that the US leads in 14 areas, is equal with the SU in 6 areas and trails in none. The report concluded that 'It will remain difficult for the USSR to close many already existing technology gaps, and new ones are likely to emerge'. (8) It is instructive to note here that this information was not included in the relevant edition of the Pentagon's annual (popular) threat assessment, Soviet Military Power. (9)

The Conventional Balance on the Central Front

In his long examination of the European conventional balance, Posen makes an important general point relating to assessing the balance. He argues: (10)

> The Warsaw Pact's and NATO's military doctrines, which determine how each alliance builds and organizes its military forces, are quite different from each other. At the most general level, the Pact prefers large numbers of major weapons and formations ... over training, the experience of military personnel, logistics, and the command, control, communications, and intelligence ... NATO, on the other hand, prefers a more balanced mix of tooth and tail, shows greater interest in the training and experience of its personnel, and places greater emphasis on tactical airpower.
>
> In terms of military operations, Pact doctrine tends to extol the advantages of the offense ... NATO tends towards a more balanced view of the relative advantages of defensive and offensive tactics ...

Figure 2.1: General Comparisons: NATO and the Warsaw Pact

Year	Military Expenditures (ME) Billion dollars		Armed Forces Thousand	Gross National Product (GNP) Billion dollars		Central Government Expenditures (CGE) Billion dollars Constant 1982
	Current	Constant 1982		Current	Constant 1982	
NATO 1983	325.1	311.9	5587	6194	5942	1969.2
Warsaw Pact 1983	299.8	287.6	5810	2564	2460	857.8

Figure 2.1: continued

	People	$\dfrac{ME}{GNP}$	$\dfrac{ME}{CGE}$	ME per capita	Armed forces per 1000 people	GNP per capita
	Million	%	%	Constant 1982 dollars		Constant 1982 dollars
NATO 1983	591.6	5.2	15.8	527	9.4	10045
Warsaw Pact 1983	383.4	11.7	33.5	750	15.2	6417

Source: World Military Expenditures and Arms Transfers, 1985 (US Arms Control and Disarmament Agency, Washington DC, 1985)

Figure 2.2: General Comparisons: United States and Soviet Union

Year	Military Expenditures (ME) Million dollars		Armed Forces Thousand	Gross National Product (GNP) Million dollars		Central Government Expenditures (CGE) Million dollars Constant 1982
	Current	Constant 1982		Current	Constant 1982	
United States						
1983	217154	208337	2222	3297800	3163913	821209
Soviet Union						
1983	258000	247525	4400	1843400	1768560	606341

18

Figure 2.2: continued

	People	ME/GNP	ME/CGE	ME per capita	Armed forces per 1000 people	GNP per capita
	Million	%	%	Constant 1982 dollars		Constant 1982 dollars
NATO 1983	234.5	6.6	25.4	888	9.5	13492
Warsaw Pact 1983	272.5	14.0	40.8	908	16.1	6490

Source: World Military Expenditures and Arms Transfers, 1985 (US Arms Control and Disarmament Agency, Washington DC, 1985)

However, that, Posen suggests, is not what is presented to the public. In his view: (11)

> ... NATO tends to buy military forces according to its own theory of victory, its own military doctrine. Analysts, however, have tended to assess the military balance according to a different - the Soviet - theory of victory. Adopting Soviet criteria for measuring the balance will always make the West look bad in comparison ...

The remainder of this section will examine Posen's claims in more detail.

Figure 2.3 presents the British Government's view, which can be regarded as a standard official assessment of the balance of forces on the central front. This clearly illustrates a Pact advantage at all of the six levels measured although in at least three of the categories the difference is so marginal that it can be discounted. This assessment, however, only tells a partial story and little use is made of the other factors that were outlined above. It is necessary, therefore, to examine and assess the implications of such factors in more detail.

A more detailed numerical assessment of the conventional balance appears each year in the International Institute for Strategic Studies (IISS) publication, The Military Balance. (12) Figure 2.4 provides these details for the 1986 edition. Like the Statement it can be deduced from the table that the WP possesses a general advantage in most of the areas analysed, excepting the case of naval forces where NATO appears to hold the advantage. The analysis provided with the table, however, is even more cautious than that provided in the Statement. It concludes (as, indeed it has done for many years) that: (13)

> ... the conventional military balance is still such as to make general military aggression a highly risky undertaking for either side. Though possession of the initiative in war will always permit an aggressor to achieve a local advantage in numbers (sufficient perhaps to allow him to believe that he might achieve limited tactical success in some areas), there would still appear to be insufficient overall strength on either side to guarantee victory ... .

Figure 2.3: The Current Balance of Forces on the Central Front (1)

	NATO	Ratio	WP
Total Soldiers	790,000	1:1.22	960,000
Soldiers in Fighting Units (2)	580,000	1:1.25	725,000
Main Battle Tanks	7,800	1:2.14	16,700
Anti-Tank Guided Weapons (3)	7,100	1:1.63	11,600
Artillery	3,000	1:3.07	9,200
Fixed Wing Tactical Aircraft	1,250	1:2.12	2,650

(1) Covers NATO forces in the Benelux countries and the Federal Republic of Germany, and Warsaw Pact forces estimated to be in Poland, Czechoslovakia and the German Democratic Republic. Includes French forces in the Federal Republic of Germany which are not declared to NATO, but excludes the Berlin garrison.
(2) Corresponds to a balance of 57 Warsaw Pact to 33 NATO divisions. Warsaw Pact divisions normally consist of fewer personnel than many NATO divisions, but contain more tanks and artillery.
(3) Crew-served systems and helicopter- or vehicle-mounted systems, but excluding those that may be fired through the gun barrel of Soviet tanks.

Source: Statement on the Defence Estimates 1987, Vol. 1 (Cm101-1, Her Majesty's Stationary Office, London, 1987), p.62.

Armoured Division Equivalents and the Bean Count

One of the major characteristics of the optimistic approach to the conventional balance is the use of an elaborate measure of combat effectiveness devised by the United States Department of Defense: (14) Armoured Division Equivalents (ADEs). This measure, introduced in 1971, weighs the mobility, survivability and firepower of all weaponry in every division on the central front. It overcomes a major limitation of the 'bean count' approach in that it attempts to take into account operational and

Figure 2.4: Conventional Force Comparisons: NATO and Warsaw Pact

NATO

	Europe North(a)	South(b)	(Spain)	US	Total (excl. Spain)
Manpower (000)					
Total uniformed manpower (e)	1,629	1,319	(320)	2,144	5,092
Reserves (all services)	2,292	2,344	(1,085)	1,683	6,319
Total ground forces	990	1,017	(230)	771	2,778
Total ground force reserves (f)	1,737	1,809	(800)	1,057	4,603
Total ground forces deployed in Europe	624	1,017	(230)	217	1,858

Warsaw Pact

	Soviet North(c)	South(d)	Non-Soviet North(c)	South(d)	Totals
Total uniformed manpower (e)	5,130		717	443	6,290
Reserves (all services)	6,265		1,181	703	8,149
Total ground forces	1,991		498	338	2,827
Total ground force reserves (f)	3,500		995	585	5,080
Total ground forces deployed in Europe	1,170 (500)	698 (65)	498	338	2,704

Ratios of NATO:Pact Totals

1:1.23
1:1.29
1:1.02
1:1.10
1:1.46

22

Figure 2.4: continued

		NATO				
		Europe				
		North(a)	South(b)	(Spain)	US	Total (excl. Spain)
<u>Divisions</u> (g)						
Divs deployed in Europe manned in peacetime	Tk (h)	12	2	-	2⅓	16⅓
	Mech	6	8	-	2⅓	16⅓
	Other	2⅓	2	-	1⅓	5⅔
Divs for reinforcement manned or on mobilization of reserves (i)	Tk	5	2	(1)	4⅔	11⅔
	Mech	13⅔	21	(1)	8⅔	43⅓
	Other	16⅓	16	(3⅔)	15⅓	46⅔
Total divs, war mobilized (h)	Tk	17	4	(1)	6	27
	Mech	21⅔	29	(1)	11	61⅔
	Other	19⅓	18	(3⅔)	16⅔	54

	Warsaw Pact				
Ratios of NATO:Pact		Soviet		Non-Soviet	
Totals	Total	North(c)	South(d)	North(c)	South (d)
1:1.94	31⅔	15	6	8	2⅔
1:2.94	48	23	9	10	6
1:1.82	10⅓	5	⅔	2⅔	2
1:2.23	26	16	4	4	2
1:1.48	64	16	26	7	15
35.0:1	1⅓	-	1⅓	-	-
1:2.14	57⅔	31	10	12	4⅔
1:1.82	112	39	35	17	21
4.76:1	11⅓	5	1⅔	2⅔	2

Figure 2.4: continued

NATO

Ground Force Equipment	Europe North(a)	Europe South(b)	(Spain)	US	Total (excl. Spain)
Main battle tanks	8,981	6,333	(883)	5,000	20,314
Arty, MRL	4,086	4,218	(1,300)	670	8,974
Mor (over 120mm)	1,760*	500*	(400)	-	2,149
SSM launchers (dual-capable)	165	6	-	216	387
ATK guns	280	-	-	-	280
ATGW launchers (crew-served, AFV-, hel-mounted)	885	126*	-	800*	1,811
AA guns	1,429	1,850*	(414)*	100	3,379
SAM launchers (crew-served ground forces only) (k)	522	100	(33)	164	786
Armed helicopters	312	174	(44)	228	714

Warsaw Pact

	Soviet North(c)	Soviet South(d)	Non-Soviet North(c)	Non-Soviet South (d)
Main battle tanks	19,500	12,700	9,770	4,640
Arty, MRL	10,000*	6,300*	4,300*	3,435*
Mor (over 120mm)	4,000*	1,000*	422*	650*
SSM launchers (dual-capable)	693	185	203	154
ATK guns	570*	420*	190	370
ATGW launchers	1,300*	1,035*	750	440
AA guns	1,100*	1,120*	1,350	1,250
SAM launchers	2,500*	1,620*	1,000	245
Armed helicopters	1,580	505	114	70

Ratios of NATO:Pact

Total	Ratio
46,610	1:2.29
24,035	1:2.68
6,072	1:2.83
1,235	1:3.19
1,550	1:5.54
3,525	1:1.95
3,525*(j)	1:1.04
5,365*(j)	1:6.83
2,085	1:2.92

Figure 2.4: continued

NATO

Naval Units	Europe North(a)	South(b)	(Spain)	US	Total (excl. Spain)
Submarines – cruise missile	–	–	–	–	–
– attack	84	48	(8)	51	183
Carriers	4	4	(1)	5	13
Cruisers	–	2	–	12	14
Destroyers	32	38	(11)	34	104
Frigates	91	51	(11)	48	190
Corvettes/large patrol craft	29	42	(18)	–	71
FAC (G/T/P)	93	55	(12)	6	154
MCM (l)	142	67	(12)	3	212
Amphibious (m)	85	140	(24)	25	250

Warsaw Pact

	Soviet North(c)	South(d)	Non-Soviet North(c)	South (d)
Submarines – cruise missile	35	2	–	3
– attack	108	40	3	3
Carriers	1	2	–	–
Cruisers	14	7	–	–
Destroyers	29	18	–	1
Frigates	33	13	3	5
Corvettes/large patrol craft	41	29	30	15
FAC (G/T/P)	45	100	76	79
MCM (l)	185	65	54	4
Amphibious (m)	73	37	35	–

Ratios of NATO:Pact

	Totals	Ratio
Submarines – cruise missile	37	–
– attack	154	1.19:1
Carriers	3	4.33:1
Cruisers	21	1:1.5
Destroyers	48	2.17:1
Frigates	54	3.52:1
Corvettes/large patrol craft	115	1:1.62
FAC (G/T/P)	300	1:1.95
MCM (l)	308	1:1.45
Amphibious (m)	145	1.72:1

25

Figure 2.4: continued

Naval and Maritime Aircraft

NATO

	Europe North(a)	Europe South(b)	(Spain)	US	Total (excl. Spain)
Bombers	-	37	-	-	37
Attack	97	10	(10)	170	277
Fighters	-	12	-	105	117
ASW	8	12	-	50	70
MR/ECM	100	36	(20)	55	191
ASW hel	238	115	(25)	30	383

Warsaw Pact

	Soviet North(c)	Soviet South(d)	Non-Soviet North(c)	Non-Soviet South(d)	Total
Bombers	100	100	-	-	200
Attack	50	100	34	-	184
Fighters	-	-	-	-	-
ASW	20	50	-	-	70
MR/ECM	99	45	10	-	154
ASW hel	30	40	-	12	82

Ratios of NATO:Pact

	Totals
Bombers	1:5.41
Attack	1.51:1
Fighters	-
ASW	1:1
MR/ECM	1.24:1
ASW hel	4.67:1

Figure 2.4: continued

NATO

Land Combat Aircraft (n)	Europe North(a)	South(b)	(Spain)	US	Total (excl. Spain)
Bombers	72	–	–	150	222
FGA	873	841	(40)	444	2,158
Fighters	118	238	(107)	96	452
Interceptors	44	–	–	18	62
Reconnaissance	142	156	(20)	51	349
ECM	(o)	(o)	(o)	(o)	(o)

Warsaw Pact

	Soviet North(c)	South(d)	Non-Soviet North(c)	South (d)	Total	Ratios of NATO:Pact
Bombers	210	–	–	–	210	1.06:1
FGA	1,025	540	421	230	2,216	1:1.03
Fighters	590	315	135	35*	1,075	1:2.38
Interceptors	(o)	(o)	810	485*	1,295	1:20.89
Reconnaissance	221	72	90	60	443	1:1.27
ECM	55	5	–	–	60	-

Notes:
* Estimated figures.
(a) Comprises Norway, Denmark, W. Germany, Luxembourg, Netherlands and Belgium, and includes forces actually deployed from Britain, Canada, US (Atlantic), France (Army; Navy; Atlantic-deployed elms incl Naval air).
(b) Comprises Turkey, Greece, Italy, Portugal, France (Navy), US Sixth Fleet and forces deployed in Southern Europe.

Figure 2.4: continued

(c) Comprises Poland, E. Germany and Czechoslovakia, and includes Soviet forces in those countries and in the Leningrad, Baltic, Belorussian and Carpathian MD.

(d) Comprises Hungary, Romania and Bulgaria, and includes Soviet forces in Hungary and in the Odessa, Kiev, North Caucasus and Trans-Caucasus MD.

(e) 'Uniformed manpower' refers to main forces only and excludes para-military forces.

(f) 'Reserves'; Many countries have Reserve obligations into middle age; where not otherwise stated in the country entry, a five-year post-conscript period has arbitrarily been selected in calculating the numbers. In Pact countries a large proportion of these older reservists are probably assigned to 'shadow' formations and units with stored obsolete equipment, potentially doubling the mobilizable forces from those shown but necessarily at very low standards of efficiency. This table, however, shows equipment totals for listed Category 1, 2 and 3 divisions only.

(g) Divisions are not a standard formation between Armies; 3 brigades or regiments are considered to be a divisional equivalent.

(h) 'Tk' includes tank and armoured divs; 'Mech' includes mechanized, motorized and motor rifle: 'Other' includes airborne, air-portable, mountain, amphibious, light infantry and naval infantry.

(i) Mobilization and reserve reinforcement systems vary considerably. A distinction between the two categories of immediate reinforcement and 'when mobilized' must of necessity be judgmental, especially for NATO. See country entries for detail.

(j) Figures in part on unit organization.

(k) Field forces only; Soviet Air Force and APVO equipment is considered primarily to be for airfield defence and not for use by field formations.

(l) Excludes support craft and inshore boats.

(m) Excludes LCU, LCVP, LCA small craft.

(n) OCU aircraft are included in these totals.

(o) Included in the figure above.

Source: The Military Balance, 1986–87 (International Institute for Strategic Studies, London, 1986).

28

qualitative differences between the two forces (it has predominantly been the case that NATO has possessed this advantage over the WP) and compares across different weapons systems (for example tanks against anti-tank systems).

The result of this approach is one considerably at variance with standard 'bean count' studies. According to official US sources the ratio stands at 1.2:1 in favour of the WP (the exact numbers of ADEs on either side is classified information) which, when taken together with the same ratio for manpower (Manpower Division Equivalent-MDE) does not indicate a situation of overwhelming superiority.

The Ground Force Balance: the Cordesman and Mako Studies

Two of the most important and perceptive studies of the ground force balance to have appeared in recent years are by the US scholars Anthony Cordesman (15) and William Mako. (16) Both take their assessments of the conventional balance further than the standard sources and, consequently, come to radically different conclusions to those hitherto presented. It is worthwhile, therefore, examining their theses in some detail.

Cordesman's View

Cordesman's analysis starts from his belief that NATO itself has a tendency to underestimate its own strengths and abilities: (17)

> NATO is unique in its tendency to underestimate its strengths. The most commonly used numbers on the NATO and Warsaw Pact balance have nothing to do with the Central Region balance or with any other balance that has military or political meaning.

Figure 2.5 provides Cordesman's view - derived from official US Congressional publications - of the Central Region Balance in 1983. (It is important to point out that Cordesman does not use ADEs measures in his calculations). From this analysis, therefore, NATO - in the most startling example - is outnumbered in committed divisions by 57 to 26. However, Cordesman later outlines the composition of the Soviet and WP divisions which has important

Figure 2.5: The Central Region Balance in 1983

	NATO			Warsaw Pact			
	US (1)	Other NATO (2)	Total	USSR(1)	Other Warsaw Pact	Total	NATO Standing
Personnel (3)	282,000	743,650	1,025,650	535,000	715,000	1,250,000	-224,350
Divisions Committed (4)							
Armor	2⅓	13	15	13	12	25	-10
Other	2⅔	8	10⅔	13	19	32	-21⅓
Total	5	21	26	26	31	57	**-31**
Ready Reinforcements (5)							
Armor	1⅔	5	6⅔	4	0	4	+2⅔
Other	11⅓	11	22⅓	4	0	4	+18⅓
Total	13	16	29	8	0	8	**+21**
Sub-Total	18	37	55	34	31	65	**-10**
First-Line Reserves (6)							
Armor	2	0	2	12	0	12	-10
Other	8	0	8	12	0	12	-4
Total	10	0	10	24	0	24	**-14**
Total Divisions	28	37	65	58	31	89	**-24**

Figure 2.5: continued

Medium Tanks (7)

Deployed	2,000	6,905	8,905	18,000	7,000	25,000	-16,095
POMCUS	1,000	0	1,000	0	0	0	+1,000
Total	3,000	6,905	9,905	18,000	7,000	25,000	**-15,095**

Tactical Aircraft (8)

Bombers	144	16	160	0	0	0	+160
Fighter/ Attack	336	1,370	1,706	530	1,000	1,530	+176
Interceptors	90	560	650	350	1,225	1,575	-925
Total	570	1,946	2,516	880	2,225	3,105	**-589**

MRBM/IRBM (9)

	0	18	18	525	0	525	**-507**

Notes:
(1) US personnel strengths are active Army and Air Force only. The Soviet side includes Category III divisions at current strengths. Soviet personnel total 410,000 in East Germany, 50,000 in Poland, and 75,000 in Czechoslovakia.
(2) French Army and Air Force totals are included in all categories, even though those forces are not under NATO control and only three divisions are deployed in Germany. Danish and German forces in the Schleswig-Holstein Province on the base of the Jutland Peninsula are technically a part of NATO's north flank, but are counted in the center sector for purposes of this comparison.

Figure 2.5: continued

(3) NATO personnel strengths are active forces only. They include 282,000 Americans, 83,500 Belgians, 5,400 Canadians, 50,000 French, 426,000 Germans (excluding forces with AFNORTH), 700 Luxembourgers, 92,100 Dutch, 65,100 British, and 20,850 Danes, a total of 1,025,650. Warsaw Pact includes Cat III divisions at current strengths. The total reflects 535,000 Soviet forces, 150,300 East Germans, 364,000 Poles, and 200,000 Czechs.

(4) Committed NATO divisions are those in West Germany. All US divisions are Army. Three CONUS-based Reforger divisions have one brigade each forward-deployed in Germany. Warsaw Pact divisions are those in East Germany, Czechoslovakia and Poland. All are Cat I. Division equivalents are excluded.

(5) US Ready Reinforcements do not conform to current contingency plans. They reflect what could be committed quickly, rather than what necessarily would: eight full Army, parts of two Reforger divisions (that show as $\frac{1}{3}$ and $\frac{2}{3}$ respectively) and two Marine Amphibious Force (MAF) division/wing teams. NATO Ready Reinforcements are six French, two Belgian, and three Dutch divisions. Soviet lists are restricted to Cat I and II divisions in the Baltic, Belorussian, and Carpathian Military Districts.

(6) First Line Reserves do not conform to current contingency plans, which contemplate withholding two or more divisions initially, including the light 82d Airborne. Instead, they reflect reinforcement by all forces in CONUS and CINCPACs Army reserve to show the best possible US case: eight Army Reserve Component divisions and two MAFs (one active, one reserve). Soviet forces are Cat III divisions in the Baltic, Belorussian, and Carpathian Military Districts.

(7) The United States has replaced all Sheridan light tanks with M-60 mediums. The number of Soviet reserve stock tanks is not ascertainable.

Figure 2.5: continued

(8) Aircraft statistics exclude US dual-based forces in CONUS. F-111s count as medium bombers. US aircraft in Great Britain and Spain show.

(9) US Pershing 1 missiles are Short Range Ballistic Missiles (SRBMs with a maximum range of about 400 miles), so do not count. The 18 'NATO' MRBMs/IRBMs are French. About one-third of Soviet MRBMs/IRBMs are in European Russia. Another third in Western Siberia could cover European targets on call.

Source: Cordesman, A.H., 'The NATO Central Region and the Balance of Uncertainty', Armed Forces Journal International, (July 1983).

Figure 2.6: Warsaw Pact Divisions, Central Region

Divisions	Total	I	Category	
			II	III
In Czechoslovakia				
Czech				
Tank	5	1	2	2
Motorized Rifle	5	3	1	1
Total	10	4	3	3
Soviet				
Tank	2	2	0	0
Motorized Rifle	3	3	0	0
Total	5	5	0	0
Grand Total	15	9	3	3
In East Germany				
East German				
Tank	2	2	0	0
Motorized Rifle	4	4	0	0
Total	6	6	0	0
Soviet				
Tank	9	9	0	0
Motorized Rifle	10	10	0	0
Total	19	19	0	0
Grand Total	25	25	0	0
In Poland				
Polish				
Tank	5	5	0	0
Motorized Rifle	8	3	2	3
Other	2	2	0	0
Total	15	10	2	3
Soviet				
Tank	2	2	0	0
Motorized Rifle	0	0	0	0
Total	2	2	0	0
Grand Total	17	12	2	3

Total Committed				
Non-Soviet				
Tank	12	8	2	2
Motorized Rifle	17	10	3	4
Other	2	2	0	0
Total	**31**	**20**	**5**	**6**
Soviet				
Tank	13	13	0	0
Motorized Rifle	13	13	0	0
Total	**26**	**26**	**0**	**0**
Grand Total	**57**	**46**	**5**	**6**
In Western Russia				
Ready Reinforcement	4	0	4	0
(all Soviet)	4	0	4	0
	8	0	8	0
First-Line Reserves	12	0	0	12
(all Soviet)	12	0	0	12
	24	0	0	24
Grand Total	**89**	**46**	**13**	**30**

Source: Cordesman, A.H., 'The NATO Central Region and the Balance of Uncertainty', Armed Forces Journal International, (July, 1983).

implications for the balance.

WP divisions are classified according to three grades of readiness. Category I are those divisions at, or around, 100 per cent capacity in both troops and equipment. Soviet Category II divisions are regarded as having full equipment potential but their personnel is only around 50-85 per cent of wartime needs. Eastern European Category II divisions have around 50-75 per cent of their expected wartime personnel and are short on some items of equipment. Finally Soviet Category III divisions have up to 35 per cent of personnel, with full equipment (most of it from Soviet stockpiles of past military production). Eastern European Category III forces '... rarely have more than 15-30 per cent of their manpower', (18) and are severely under-equipped.

Figure 2.6 provides Cordesman's breakdown, by category and country, of the WP divisions in the central region. When this is compared to his previous analysis it highlights how Pact strength is less than shown by the standard 'bean count' approach. For example, of the Pact's 57 committed divisions, whilst 26 Soviet and 20 East European divisions are Category I, the remaining eleven are comprised of Categories II and III forces. Furthermore, the Pact's ready-reinforcement divisions are all Soviet Category II and its frontline reserves all Soviet Category III divisions. Finally, as will be emphasised later in this Chapter, the SU may not feel too confident of the reliability of the Polish and Czechoslovakian forces. When one considers that they contribute fourteen of the committed Category I divisions and all eleven of the committed Category II and III forces the balance begins to look more even.

The final point to make here, and one not included in Cordesman's analysis, is the size of Soviet divisions compared to their US and West German equivalents. Soviet divisions tend to be considerably smaller. In his assessment of the conventional balance Kaufmann commented in relation to this point: (19)

> ... if US and Soviet divisions are compared, an average US division is nearly 40 per cent larger in manpower; the division slice (or the division with a prorated share of Corps, army, and support forces) is probably more than twice as large ... .

Thus manpower counts on the central front tend to be relatively equal (see Figure 2.4) despite the nominal difference in divisions.

Defence and Reinforcements: Mako's Analysis

One of the crucial questions left open by Cordesman is whether NATO might possess sufficient forces to deal with a Pact attack but be unable to use them effectively. This question concerns the relative ability of NATO and the WP to get its forces and equipment to the central front area quickly in the event of a crisis. This problem was considered by Mako in his Brookings Institution study US Ground Forces and the Defense of Central Europe. (20) In the second section of his study Mako gives a detailed review of what he suggests is official US contingency planning for Pact attacks on the central front (the area linked to this - the relative advantages of the defence over the offence - is dealt with below). In Mako's view: (21)

For planning purposes, the US Defense Department appears to focus on four possible contingencies: a two-front attack or a three-front attack by forces based in Eastern Europe, an attack reinforced from the three westernmost military districts of the Soviet Union, and an attack augmented by forces from additional Soviet military districts.

It is clear that these forces would take different times to mobilise and by looking at the NATO forces which would become available during these periods, it will be possible to get a better idea of the force ratios which would apply in different kinds of attack. It will therefore be possible to examine the question left open by Cordesman's more static analysis as to whether NATO might have enough forces in principle but not enough to apply them in practice.

The four scenarios of attack suggested by Mako are as follows:

(a) A two-front attack: Using the Group of Soviet Forces in Germany (GSFG), the Soviet Central Group Forces (CGF) in Czechoslovakia and the East German Army. The time taken to organise such an attack has been estimated at as little as two days by US Senators Nunn and Bartlett, eight days by General Haig and four days by Mako himself, using a conservative estimate.

(b) A three-front attack: Using the above forces plus Polish, Czechoslovakian and Soviet Northern Group forces (NGF). Mobilisation estimates range from 8-15 days with Mako suggesting a conservative compromise of 11 days. Polish and Czechoslovakian participation might be questionable in this scenario, but they contribute 40 per cent of combat potential.

(c) A six-front attack: Forces from the Baltic, Belorussian and Carpathian military districts of the USSR would be added to those recorded above. Mobilisation estimates include six weeks, four weeks (Mako) and two weeks. Polish and Czechoslovakian forces would contribute 25 per cent of the combat potential.

(d) An augmented six-front attack: As above, but with the likely addition of divisions from the Kiev, Moscow, Volga, Ural and Central Asian military districts. Mobilisation estimates range from 4 weeks, 60 days (Mako) to three months. Over half the divisions involved would be category II and III and Polish and

37

Figure 2.7: Mako's Four Attack Scenarios: Manpower and ADE Ratios

Scenario	Mobilisation Time	WP MDEs	NATO MDEs	MDEs Ratio	WP ADEs	NATO ADEs	ADEs Ratio
2-front attack	M+3	21	26	1:1.2	24	21.8	1.1:1
	M+5	21	31	1:1.5	24	25.8	1:1.1
3-front attack	M+10	38	38	1:1	40	32.6	1.2:1
	M+14	38	39	1:1.0	40	33.0	1.2:1
6-front attack	M+28	59	40	1.5:1	61	34.3	1.8:1
	M+42	59	43	1.4:1	61	36.8	1.7:1
augmented 6-front attack	M+75	80	48	1.7:1	81	43.0	1.9:1
	M+90	80	51	1.6:1	81	45.8	1.8:1

Note: M = Mobilisation day

Source: Mako, W.P. U.S. Ground Forces and the Defense of Central Europe, (The Brookings Institution, Washington, D.C. 1983).

Czechoslovakian divisions would contribute 20 per cent of the combat potential.

Mako then goes on to estimate the numbers of ADEs and MDEs which could be deployed by both forces in the above scenarios. Figure 2.7 compares available Pact forces with NATO using these measures. The 'quicker' mobilisation times noted above have not been examined as Mako is sceptical that the Pact could achieve appropriate rates of organisation and deployment.

From Mako's analysis it is clear that NATO is in a far better position to defend itself than hitherto officially thought. The overall ADEs for both the two- and three-front attacks clearly remain on or below 1.2:1 and NATO should be able to defend itself under such conditions. For the six-front attacks the ratio of forces approaches but never exceeds 2:1, reaching its highest level of 1.9:1 at the beginning of the six-front attack scenario.

The viability of NATO's conventional position, which these figures demonstrate, is further reinforced by the fact that Mako makes a rather cautious estimate of the total number of ADEs which could become available from the United States under any of the above contingencies. The Cordesman figures for US forces produce more ADEs capability because in his assessment: (22)

US Ready Reinforcements do not conform to current contingency plans. They reflect what could be committed quickly rather than what necessarily would ... .

Taking this into account Mako perhaps leaves out nearly nine ADEs which the US could deploy on the front line. Therefore, although the ADEs ratios arrived at by Mako (Figure 2.7) remain below 2:1, NATO's position is still more favourable due to the availability of US reinforcements not included in his estimate.

The Balance of Air Power

Whilst ADEs provides an indication of qualitative differences in ground combat forces, there are also significant qualitative factors in the balance of air power. As was seen in Figure 2.3 the British Statement claims that, in terms of fixed-wing tactical aircraft, the WP possesses an advantage of over 2:1. (23) The first important point to make here is that on both sides there are a number of aircraft deployed either away from the front line or on ships which could be quickly transported to Europe in the event of a crisis and which are excluded from the total listed. This was the subject of a Parliamentary question in May 1985 from Mr J.P. Ashdown MP and it is worth quoting question and answer in full: (24)

> Mr Ashdown asked the Secretary of State for Defence what information he has as to the total number of (a) North Atlantic Treaty Organisation and (b) Warsaw pact land-based and maritime aircraft based in the North Atlantic Treaty Organisation area.

> Mr Lee: The total number of fixed wing combat aircraft both land and sea based in or facing NATO Europe or the NATO sea areas is as follows:

> NATO   4900
> Warsaw Pact   8100

> Additionally, there are some 1,750 NATO combat aircraft presently based in the United States and Canada.

Therefore, by including this substantial additional capability of 1750 combat aircraft in the NATO totals, the balance is much closer than suggested in the Statement. Furthermore, a report by the Carnegie Foundation (25) on conventional forces argued that, whilst the Pact possesses an advantage of around 2:1 in the numbers of combat aircraft in central Europe, when measured in terms of bomb tonnage (payload) NATO holds the advantage. The relevant figures at 100 miles is 3:1 in NATO's favour and at 200 miles the advantage is substantially higher at 7:1. Thus by combining the above two factors - the deployment of reserve forces and overall aircraft capability - it is possible to argue that in the crucial area of military measurement (that of effectiveness) NATO aircraft are superior.

The findings of the Carnegie Foundation have been endorsed in Epstein's (26) detailed study of the Soviet air threat to Europe. Here, even when the author used optimistic assessments of Soviet strength, the West was still seen to hold the advantage.

Finally, however, the question of air superiority, when applied to the situation on the central front, can be judged to be an academic one. Commenting on the air figures produced in the NATO publication NATO and the Warsaw Pact: Force Comparisons (27) (which highlighted glaring 'deficiencies' on the part of NATO's forces) Cordesman commented: (28)

> These NATO air figures seem a bit thick even for comparisons designed to serve the purposes of political gamesmanship. They include most of the strategic defense forces of the Warsaw Pact - which almost certainly would not be committed in bulk to any attack on NATO even under the worst conditions - and ignore America's impressive ability to deploy tactical air power based in the US.

In fact there is a larger problem: (29)

> They ignore the fact that both sides would be short of air bases, air base protection, and support during the initial phases of any conflict. The issue is how many sorties can be supported in the forward area. Both sides have more aircraft than they can effectively deploy in the first 30 days of a conflict.

Thus, when an extensive examination of the Soviet air threat to Europe is considered, it is possible to argue that NATO is certainly not at the disadvantage standard sources claim and, indeed, may hold the advantage.

A Note on Naval Forces

Although consideration of naval forces is strictly outside the scope of the present study, it is worthwhile to briefly examine the position as it does have an important bearing on the overall balance. The SU have been seen as having a navy of overwhelming size with the ability to project power worldwide. Indeed, the SU has long presented this view of its navy, however 'enhanced' it is eventually judged to be. This was particularly the case under the long reign of Admiral Gorshkov. (30)

However, other analyses have tended to see the position

differently from governmental accounts. For example, in the table reproduced in Figure 2.4 from the IISS, NATO can be seen to hold an overall advantage over the Pact in most areas of the naval balance. This view has been endorsed in a report by the Heritage Foundation which found that '... the US Navy still maintains a wide lead over its Soviet counterpart ... (31) Furthermore, in their report cited above, the Carnegie Foundation found that generally the advantage lay with the West: (32)

> ... NATO navies have a considerable lead over Warsaw Pact navies in numbers of aircraft carriers, major surface combatants (frigates, destroyers, and cruisers), and amphibious warfare ships. The Warsaw Pact navies lead in numbers of general purpose submarines, minor surface combatants (coastal defence ships below 1,000 tons), and mine warfare ships.

> ... (There is) an overwhelming NATO lead in aggregate tonnage. This is important because the tonnage, or size, of warships gives some indication of capabilities. Larger ships tend to have greater ranges, be more sustainable in combat, and have the capacity to carry a greater number of weapon systems.

The final point to make, however, - as in so many questions relating to force assessments - is whether such forces would perform effectively in combat. In NATO's case this particularly refers to the ability of NATO's forces and equipment to get to the combat area. In relation to this point Kaufman comments that in terms of standard military analyses '... essential tonnage for NATO would get through and the threat to the sea lines of communication would be contained'. (33)

Defence Versus Offence

It has often been stated that in military strategy a well prepared defence holds the advantage over the offence. There is no reason to suggest - apart from the unlikely possibility of an effective Pact surprise 'bolt from the blue' attack - that the position is any different when applied to the prevailing situation on the central front.
　　The basis of NATO's strategic planning in Europe is that

the Alliance would never place itself in the position of invading Eastern Europe and that it is the SU and WP which has a commitment to offensive strategies. It may be regarded as doubtful, given the SU's past history, its inability to end the conflict in Afghanistan and the problems in maintaining the Eastern European empire that it would wish to place itself in the position of occupying Western Europe. However, in terms of the present study, that question can be left aside.

In his study of the theory and practice of conventional deterrence and defence Mearsheimer (34) provides an account of how NATO, even facing an imbalance in total numbers, would still retain an advantage by holding the position of the defence.

As can be seen in Figure 2.8, in its strategy of forward defence NATO defends an approximate 800 kilometre perimeter on the inner-German border. Here, NATO's forces (Allied Forces Central Europe - AFCENT) are divided 'layer-cake' style into eight Corps sectors comprising forces from five NATO countries. The Northern Army Group (NORTHAG) which defends the North German Plain avenue of attack, consists of Dutch, West German, Belgian and British forces (the British Army on the Rhine); the Central Army Group (CENTAG), which defends the Fulda Gap and Hof Corridor avenues of attack, consists of two Corps from West Germany and two from the United States.

In his study Mearsheimer (35) considers three scenarios in assessing the ability of the West to counter a Pact attack. Firstly, the standing start attack in which, after little mobilisation, the Pact attacks an unprepared NATO. The second is where NATO detects the Pact mobilisation but fails to counter-mobilise for fear of triggering a Pact attack. Whilst not discounting these two scenarios (although the first is regarded as being highly unlikely) Mearsheimer claims it is the third scenario which is of importance in any analysis of conventional deterrence. This is where the Pact attempts to carry out a successful blitzkrieg strategy in Europe after the Pact had mobilised and NATO had counter-mobilised. As was emphasised earlier, at the onset of a period of mobilisation the ratio in terms of both ADEs and MDEs is 1.2:1 in the Pact's favour. Mearsheimer comments: (36)

> If NATO begins mobilising its forces before the Pact does, or simultaneously, then the force ratios will

Figure 2.8: Corps Sectors of Military Responsibility on NATO's Central Front.

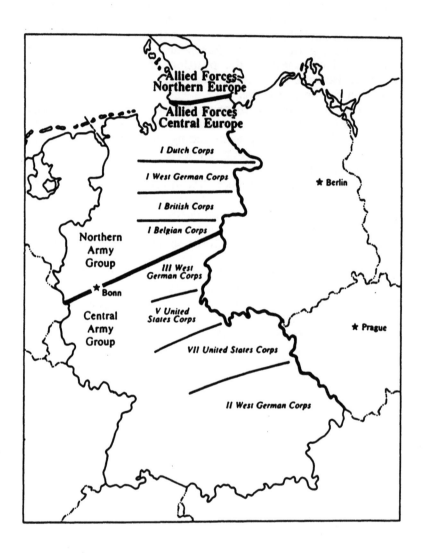

Sources: Congressional Budget Office, <u>U.S. Ground Forces: Design and Cost Alternatives for NATO and Non-NATO Contingencies</u>, prepared by P. Hillier, and N. Slatkin (CBO, 1980), p.11; and <u>Aviation Week and Space Technology</u>, June 7, 1982, p.57.

remain close to 1.2:1 (in armoured division equivalents) and 1.36:1 (in divisional manpower) ... If NATO starts mobilising a few days after the Pact, then the balance of forces should approach but not exceed a 2:1 ratio in the very early days of mobilisation and should then fall to a level close to the premobilisation ratios.

In considering whether such forces would be sufficient to offset a Pact attack, Mearsheimer takes a hypothetical (but probably reasonable) case in which the Pact has 64 ADEs and NATO 32: a ratio of 2:1.

In assessing whether a blitzkrieg would be successful it is usually assumed that an attacker needs an advantage of around 3-5:1 at the point of attack. Indeed in a recent study Martin has claimed that Soviet doctrine: '... calls for amassing at least a 5:1 superiority in major armaments before launching an offensive.' (37) One of Mearsheimer's examples is where the Pact wanted a 4:1 advantage at four dispersed points, with NATO being spread evenly across its front. The situation which would then obtain is shown in Figure 2.9. Mearsheimer concludes from this that: (38)

> ... as long as NATO keeps the overall force ratio under 2:1, it is impossible for the Soviets to have six-ten axes of advance and at the same time to have an overwhelming advantage in forces on each axis (that is, a ratio of 4:1 or more). The Soviets simply do not have a great enough overall force advantage to allow them to spread out their forces on numerous widely dispersed axes.

In addition the Pact would leave open considerable gaps which NATO could exploit.

There are two other factors which can be mentioned here: firstly the question of force-to-space ratios and, secondly, the crossing-the-T phenomenon. Regarding the question of force-to-space ratios, Mearsheimer states that, in general, a brigade can best hold a front that is around 7-15 kilometres long. In the NORTHAG section 30 brigades are responsible for around 225 kilometres; even allowing here for the traditional 'two brigades up, and one back', each brigade would have to cover 11 kilometres. In the more difficult terrain of the CENTAG sections (see below) 33 brigades cover around 500 kilometres; each brigade there is responsible for around 15 kilometres. Thus, even where the

Figure 2.9: Distribution of Forces when Soviets Desire a 4:1 Advantage

	NATO		- Central Front -	WP	
Northag	4	div	16	div
	4	div	0	div
	4	div	16	div
	4	div	0	div
Centag	4	div	16	div
	4	div	0	div
	4	div	16	div
	4	div	0	div
Total	32	div	64	div

Source: Mearsheimer, J., Conventional Deterrence, (Cornell University Press, London, 1983), p.174.

Pact attack is most likely to come - across the North German Plain - the defence seems adequate and even though the area covered is larger in the CENTAG region, the terrain is with the defender. In addition, reinforcements could become quickly available. The second point relates to what is known as the crossing-the-T phenomenon. (39) This states that even if a major force ratio advantage is built up at a point on the front, the defender still retains the advantage as not all the attacking forces can be put into operation at the point of attack, simply due to the lack of room.

Geographical Factors in the Central Region

A related point to the above, and one which again highlights the advantages for the West, concerns the geographical factors in the region. In terms of the actual areas of attack on the central front NATO can be said to hold the advantage. Wicker has commented: (40)

> None of these attack routes ... would be easily traversed; most present obstacles - canals, bogs, the extensive Hanover urban sprawl on the North German Plain, narrow winding mountain passages for the two

corridors. The Fulda Gap between two mountain ranges is at most points only 20-30 kilometres wide, not advantageous for attack against prepared defences.

Figure 2.10 shows the major attack routes in the central region. With only four possible areas of attack NATO can concentrate its forces directly there. The CENTAG border areas (with the exception of a few corridors near Fulda) are heavily wooded and rugged. Forests cover approximately 29 per cent of the FRG and this is increasing slightly each year through government programmes. In addition, around 9 per cent of the land is built-up and this urban sprawl is expected to increase over the next few years. Finally, there are a substantial number of villages; in general every 12 square kilometres contains a village with under 3000 inhabitants.

With reference to the possible avenues of attack it is again possible to conclude that the advantage lies with the West. The North German Plain - acknowledged to be the most likely attack route - is the flattest of the three although, in addition to Wicker's point above, there are a number of rivers, canals and bogs which (particularly under wet conditions) would impede a blitzkrieg attack. In the Gottingen Corridor there is some forestation and the attacking forces would have to tackle the Leine and Weser Rivers. The Fulda Gap, which leads to Frankfurt, offers few obstacles although an attacker would have to traverse the Fulda River and, finally, the Hof Corridor has the most difficult terrain and is substantially more obstacle-ridden than the others.

Alliance Reliability: the Question of the Eastern European Forces

The final factor it is necessary to include in a comprehensive net threat assessment is a consideration of the reliability of allies. Whilst this factor is possibly the most difficult to assess its inclusion is necessary in the formulation of defence policy.

For the Western Alliance, apart from French idiosyncracy, the reliability of the other NATO countries can be regarded as reasonably secure. With the WP, however, it is not possible to be so certain. Some authors (41) have pointed to the likely problems that the SU would face with some of the Eastern European countries. For

47

Figure 2.10: Likely Avenues of Attack in the NATO Central Region

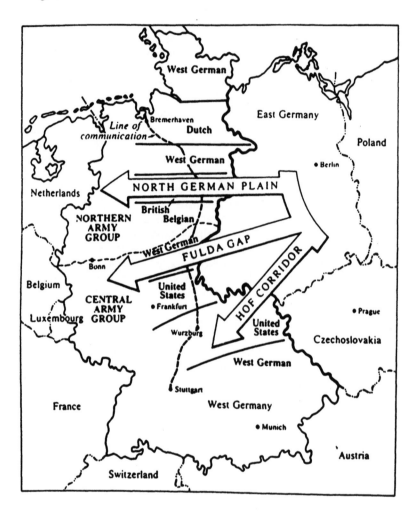

Sources: Lawrence, R.D. and J. Record, <u>U.S. Force Structure in NATO: An Alternative</u> (Brookings Institution, 1974), p.31; and Congressional Budget Office, <u>U.S Ground Forces: Design and Cost Alternatives for NATO and Non-NATO Contingencies</u>, prepared by P. Hillier and N. Slatkin (CBO, 1980), p.11.

example, whilst the Bulgarians - being the SU's most trusted ally - would support a Soviet attack (although they are one of the weakest members of the Pact and have limited military experience), for other Pact countries the position is far from clear.

It might be regarded as doubtful that East German troops would wish to fight West Germans, and Romania would almost certainly attempt to continue her policy of relative independence throughout a conflict. Even with the other allies the SU could not be too confident of support: both Hungary and Czechoslovakia have been invaded by the SU over the past thirty years and considerable anti-Soviet sentiment remains. Finally, Poland has friendly relations with a number of Western countries, although its traditional enemy is Germany.

The Soviet's problem may be further compounded by fears that some Eastern European countries would attempt secession from the Soviet Bloc during a conflict: thus not only would the Pact have lost the support of an ally but a substantial number of forces would have to be diverted to quell the rebellion. Indeed, this fear of losing allies and, more particularly, parts of the SU through internal revolutions in a period of international conflict, has been suggested as one of the main reasons why the Pact stresses the importance of winning a war quickly. The longer a war with NATO persisted, the more difficult it would be to retain control over the Soviet Bloc. (42) Finally, there is the possibility of China and/or the US opening a second front against the SU during a war.

The major factor in all of this would be the ability or otherwise of the SU to persuade its allies that it was in their national interest to attack NATO. The problem with worst-case analyses of the standard kind is that they assume all WP countries would take part; as pointed out above, however, a rational assessment needs to be far more cautious.

Thus, in a comprehensive assessment the conventional balance on the central front is nowhere as difficult for NATO as is traditionally suggested. The numerical differences (when expressed in ADEs) are marginal and NATO possesses the advantages of the defence. It is clear from this that the Pact would have considerable difficulty in undertaking a successful invasion of the West.

STRENGTHENING CONVENTIONAL DETERRENCE (1): THE FOFA CONCEPT AND AIRLAND BATTLE DOCTRINE

Against this background of a more optimistic assessment of the conventional balance it can be argued that it is possible for NATO to substantially reassess the role of both its nuclear and conventional forces. Indeed, if the assessment of the balance presented above is acceptable, it is clear that NATO could move to a radically different form of defence in central Europe and one which did not rely on the threat of nuclear first-use. However where changes in policy have occurred these have been in terms of strengthening conventional forces <u>within</u> the parameters of flexible response. Thus, NATO has reduced the stockpiles of some nuclear weapons deployed in Europe, but these have had little effect on the balance and no effect on nuclear policy. Furthermore, whilst such changes have made NATO able to fight a war more effectively, they have contributed nothing to lessen the likelihood of war occurring and, indeed, may have actually worsened the position, particularly in terms of crisis management and the problems of pre-emption in a period of crisis (this is discussed in more detail below).

There are two principal changes: firstly, the introduction of Airland Battle (the US Army Doctrine) and, secondly, the development of NATO's FOFA concept. These will now be examined in a little more detail.

Airland Battle: Airland Battle is the official doctrine of the United States Army at Corps level and below. It has some links with FOFA although it is substantially different in a number of important areas. Airland Battle represents a move away from the war of attrition which is expected to develop in a conflict under the current policy of forward defence and favours a manoeuvre strategy. It employs the idea of the extended battlefield (in terms of range, time and possible targets), plans for the integrated use of conventional, nuclear and chemical weapons, and has the capacity for pre-emptive action. Like FOFA, Airland Battle calls for offensive action against enemy targets, although in this case it is between 30 and 150km from the forward edge of battle.

Follow on Forces Attack (FOFA): The FOFA concept became an official part of NATO policy in November 1984. FOFA has as its principal objective the destruction, or delay, of the Warsaw Pact's second echelon (follow-on) forces, which would follow the main attack as reinforcements and replacements and seize any areas left by the first attacking force. (NATO has always had a deep interdiction strategy of this nature; the difference with FOFA being that rather than relying on manned aircraft to carry out this role, as at present, new missiles and sophisticated targetting systems will be used.) The implementation of FOFA in a conflict would involve the destruction of both mobile and fixed targets inside Eastern Europe at least 400 km from the forward edge of the battle and up to, and including, the three Westernmost military districts of the Soviet Union. FOFA expects to exploit the new emerging - deep strike - technologies, although at present the weapons available to undertake FOFA are deployed on manned aircraft. However, it is eventually intended to deploy conventionally armed deep strike weapons which would include, for example, cruise, Lance and Pershing missiles armed with conventional warheads.

Despite their obvious differences, not least in their planned employment of nuclear and chemical weapons, both FOFA and Airland Battle are currently planned for use in Europe. (Rather confusingly, all the nations deploying forces on the central front have their own doctrine and train according to that doctrine.) Despite this, General Rogers has claimed that all NATO's forces: (43)

> ... which would come under SACEUR's command in the event of war would operate under an ACE (Allied Command Europe) Chain of Command and ACE policies, doctrines and concepts - not those of any single Alliance nation.

This may change, however, with the likely adoption of Airland Battle as an Alliance doctrine. As Weinberger reported to Congress in June 1984: (44)

> ... both the Army and Air Force are engaged in continuous bilateral discussions with their several Allied counterpart services. These discussions have already produced and will continue to produce, modifications ... which will eventually be incorporated

51

in agreed Alliance doctrinal statements. We are satisfied that in the case of the Airland Battle doctrine, that process is proceeding as it should.

Thus, it seems that NATO may be moving in the direction of adopting Airland Battle in addition to the FOFA concept. It is worth, therefore, examining briefly the implications of FOFA as, firstly, some of these are equally applicable to Airland Battle and, secondly, they do highlight some of the considerable problems relating to issues of necessity, crisis management, costs, and the failure to raise the nuclear threshold which the Alliance is now getting involved in.

Implications of FOFA

There are five principal implications of FOFA. Firstly, it would seem that there is some dispute as to whether striking deep is the most appropriate response to a Pact attack. In NATO Review, (45) Greenwood claimed that the Pact is now placing more emphasis on initial operations on the front line and that striking at these targets rather than striking deep might be more effective. Secondly, there is some doubt that the new systems will work. Whilst extensive tests have been carried out, these have tended to be under favourable conditions. Weinberger himself recognised this when he admitted in June 1984 that '... much of the technology now becoming available is still relatively immature, and little of it is operationally proven.' (46)

FOFA would also involve considerable increases in defence expenditure. General Rogers has suggested that the emerging technologies required for deep strike operations can be purchased for a real annual increase of 4 per cent in defence budgets. According to Greenwood, (47) however, in the Autumn of 1984 General Rogers upgraded his assessment to an annual real increase of 7 per cent. However, only four NATO countries have been able to meet the previous agreed commitment to an annual real increase of 3 per cent. Thus, unless there are substantial reductions in other areas of defence expenditure, it is doubtful that most NATO countries will be able to honour an increase of the level required. For Britain this problem is acute. It is clear, as the Select Committee on Defence reported, (48) that Britain has far too many commitments for its available budget, a situation which will undoubtedly worsen as the zero-growth budget is implemented. The most likely impact of this (if the commitment to the Trident submarine force is maintained) will be a severe cutback in conventional forces.

It is the final two implications that are the most important. Although one of the desired aims of adopting FOFA is to raise the nuclear threshold, it is not clear that this would be the case. FOFA makes no change in the existing policy of nuclear first-use and the deployment of cruise and Pershing is planned to continue. In addition, there is the considerable problem of pre-emption: the use of the deep strike technologies is expected to be early in a conflict as it is at this point that they would have the most impact. As a consequence, it is these weapons that the Pact would aim to take out in some form of pre-emptive strike. (The opposite could also occur: NATO, perceiving a Pact mobilisation, and fearing a pre-emptive strike, may launch their own strike.) The problem is compounded by some of the planned deep strike missiles being dual capable. The Pact would have great difficulty, for example, in deciding if a cruise, Pershing or Lance missile is armed with a conventional or nuclear warhead and as some of the warheads planned for use have a similar explosive capability to low-yield nuclear weapons, the dangers of miscalculation increase. Facing this, the Pact may launch its own nuclear strike in pre-empting the West. Thus, rather than raising the nuclear threshold, FOFA may significantly lower it. (49) In addition, the prospects of effective crisis management are significantly reduced.

The final implication, and one equally as important, is that the development and deployment of the deep strike weapons may lead to a conventional arms race in Europe. The Pact would almost certainly develop their own countermeasures (50) to the NATO deployments and a conventional arms race would ensue.

FOFA and Airland Battle commit the West to dangerous and destabilising strategies which do little to enhance conventional deterrence. When measured against the objectives outlined earlier in this paper it is clear that they do not contribute to the longer-term raising of the nuclear threshold. Finally, as Ned Lebow recently emphasised, it is ironic: (51)

> ... that many American military officers and defense intellectuals are attracted to offensive strategies at a time when an effort should be made to dissuade the

> Soviets from their commitment to the offensive. Surely, if there is anything more dangerous than one side committed to an offensive strategy, it would be both sides committed to it. Such a situation would dramatically intensify East-West tensions and make the contemporary security dilemma in Europe even more reminiscent of the situation that prevailed in the years before 1914. It would also constitute folly to the extreme, for ... offensive strategies are not only destabilising but quite contrary to the real interests of both superpowers.

Thus, as both FOFA and Airland Battle are clearly inadequate to the current situation it is perhaps time that change was made in a different direction.

STRENGTHENING CONVENTIONAL DETERRENCE (2): A NON-PROVOCATIVE DEFENSIVE DETERRENCE STRATEGY

Because of the limitations (and clear dangers) of prevailing NATO policy the Alliance should now consider moving towards a radically different form of defence. Various proposals have been outlined over the past few years for a Western defence which moves away from the reliance on nuclear forces. (52) Many of these can be summarised in the proposed strategy of non-provocative defensive deterrence. This form of defence would rely heavily on conventional weaponry, seek to highlight its defensive nature and would not threaten Eastern Europe with major counter-offensives.

Before moving on to a more detailed discussion of the areas where NATO's defence could be enhanced within defensive deterrence it is worth mentioning two major factors: the questions of NATO and the role of the counter-attack against a Warsaw Pact invasion.

A strategy of defensive deterrence should develop, where possible, within the NATO context; at the present time there seem few alternatives to maintaining the framework of collective security. A country intent on promoting the adoption of defensive deterrence will have more potential influence if it remained a member of NATO than if it left it. In addition, there would be clear problems if the Alliance began to break up which could create a more destabilising situation than currently exists. For example, if

Britain were to announce it was to leave NATO the US might itself decide to leave and create a fortress America. Similarly, the FRG may choose to develop its own nuclear capability. Correspondingly, however, a continued membership of NATO should not be taken for granted. If there was a clear sign of intransigence in changing NATO policy among the Alliance then alternative policies would need to be considered. These could include, for example, a move towards a non-aligned position or the creation of a European defence alliance.

The second factor relates to the question of a counter-attack capability within defensive deterrence. Whilst the priority within such a strategy should be a reliance on weaponry that exhibits, as far as it is possible, its defensive nature (no weapon is unambiguous to the extent of being seen as totally defensive) it may be necessary, as the ADC (53) highlighted, to retain some limited counter-attack capability to disrupt Soviet reinforcements and supplies. However, such weaponry, (which would principally be the maintenance of a small force of tanks and long-range missiles and bombers) would need to be deployed well back from the front line and targetted at Soviet, rather than East European, forces.

Elements of the New Strategy

In addition to the factors cited above the literature now available on transforming NATO's defences has highlighted four principal elements in a strategy of defensive deterrence: firstly, a major reliance on non-nuclear forces; secondly, a strengthening of Allied Forces Central Europe (AFCENT); thirdly, the creation of a barrier defence and, fourthly, an increase in prepositioned supplies and war stocks. These will now be examined in more detail.

A Reliance on Non-Nuclear Forces

A strategy of defensive deterrence in Europe should be based around non-nuclear forces. It can be argued that an immediate move to a policy of no-first-use of nuclear weapons together with the removal of all battlefield nuclear weapons should be instituted. It would then be essential to reverse the INF modernisation programme and remove all nuclear components from dual-capable systems.

There then arises the potential problem of nuclear blackmail which has been seen by some as being a prime obstacle to moving away from a nuclear-based defence. However, whilst nuclear blackmail may be seen as a possible method of exerting pressure on a non-nuclear power, it is doubtful this would be the case in practice. Booth, (54) for example, has argued that coercion through nuclear blackmail has been a rare occurrence in the past and is likely to remain so. If it were used, however, not only would the action have implications for the allies of the threatening nation but it would also provide a major argument for proliferation, neither of which would be of benefit to the SU. In addition, the SU would still face the nuclear capability of the US which, even if no longer formally allied to Western Europe, would be unlikely to sit idly by. Finally, at its most basic level, Booth (55) argues that the risks of nuclear blackmail - however small - are preferable to the risks involved in current defence policy.

Strengthening of AFCENT

Within a strategy of defensive deterrence the prevailing strategy of forward defence should be maintained (although made considerably less rigid) and a more flexible policy of defence in depth introduced. Tillson (56) has proposed the creation of a defensive zone in the FRG which would average 40 kilometres wide and extend around 860 kilometres from the North Sea to the Austrian border. This would require, in geographical terms, 32,000 square kilometres (see below for the discussion on a barrier defence). In addition, if the threat from the Pact is so large, then it is surely necessary to make major structural changes to CENTAG and NORTHAG (see Figure 2.8). Such changes could include, for example, a simple swapping round of NORTHAG and CENTAG forces. This could ensure that the stronger forces are set against the most likely attack route.

An additional area where NATO could enhance its conventional components is through the greater use of reserve forces. Canby has commented: (57)

> ... the critical deficiency of NATO has always been the lack of combat units and operational reserves ... NATO Europe has sufficient manpower, and even a sufficient number of trained reservists, but it has never placed these reservists into organised units nor bought the

necessary material to equip them.

Mako (58) has estimated that out of the reserve establishments of France, Belgium, the FRG and the Netherlands (which numbered in 1980 a total of 1,126,000 troops) only 158,000 were assigned to major reserve combat units. Martin (59) has estimated that NATO could have available, at mobilisation day plus 90, an additional 930,000 European troops '... if organised into units and released from home defence duties.' (60) This amounts to around 40 per cent of NATO's total forces.

In addition, Hamilton's (61) examination of NATO's reserve military manpower has argued that the effective use of reserve forces would both redress what he sees as a conventional imbalance in favour of the Warsaw Pact and accomplish this without involving excessive costs: (62)

> ... NATO conventional capabilities can be strengthened dramatically by equipping and reorganising available trained European military manpower to form new operational combat units. (Most of these new formations would be reserve units.) If this were done, the gap between NATO conventional forces and NATO requirements could be erased at a relatively modest cost.

Large reserve levels could be adapted for various duties and responsibilities. Canby (63) has suggested that they could be used for building up divisional strengths particularly for use in support functions.

In addition to this both Canby (64) and Loser (65) have proposed that light infantry units armed with modern anti-tank weapons and capable of rapid manoeuvre could be deployed. These could be placed along the central front and could channel the Pact attack and mask any local counter-offensive.

A final area where NATO's forces could be restructured is through an organisational change in Western European countries' armed forces. This is related to Cordesman's (66) point earlier regarding the excessive numbers of NATO and Pact aircraft and the shortage of air bases. Thus, if the Dutch, Belgian, Danish and German air forces were reduced by 450 planes this could release additional finance for improved ground forces. (67) Such a lost capability could be offset by the US which has more combat aircraft available than can be accommodated in the overcrowded European air bases. Figure 2.11 outlines the US air reserve capability in 1980. This proposal also has the added attraction of enhancing NATO's conventional defences without involving large increases in defence expenditure.

Figure 2.11: US Air Reserve 1980-1

	Wings	Squadrons	Aircraft
Air National Guard	24	91	1570
US Air Force Reserve	17	53	489
US Naval Reserve	-	45	394
US Marine Corps Reserve	-	-	300
Aircraft Total			2753

Source: Brayton, A.A., 'American Mobilisation Plans for the 1980s', RUSI Journal of the Royal United Services Institute, (March 1981), p.330.

The Creation of a Barrier Defence

A major innovation that has been proposed as a potential component in defensive deterrence is the creation of a barrier defence. Indeed, it has been regarded as a considerable failing in current strategy that barriers and fortifications do not play a role in the defence of the West. As Keegan (68) has commented, '... it is an almost bizarre hiatus in the NATO defense system that no fortifications have been constructed on its fronts'. Indeed, it is clear that such measures represent both an economical and effective aid to the defence. Kaufmann, (69) for example, has claimed that standard military data indicates the effective use of barriers could reduce a Pact attack by up to 40 per cent. Similarly, Freeman (70) has argued that obstacles deployed along the central front could reduce an attacker to a third of his original speed and increase his casualty rates by up to 60 per cent.

There would be various elements in a barrier defence utilising both natural and artificial obstacles. Cross (71) has outlined some of the initial preparations which could be made in creating a barrier defence in the FRG: (72)

All railways running across the front should have their

cuttings/embankments landscaped to enhance their stopping power. Similarly, all rivers and canals should have their banks cut to deny armour easy access and should, wherever possible, be made sufficiently wide to stop a 'bounce' crossing. All construction work throughout the zone involving walled terracing, recreation and irrigation lakes, ditches and hedgerows should be coordinated to augment the natural obstacle line. Forestation should also be planned to ensure impenetrability to armour, all fire-breaks being earmarked for blockage by anti-tank ditches or embankments. Finally, all roads and railways, canals and river lines, should be prechambered for easy demolition using conventional explosives to deny their use to the enemy and, in so doing, create more obstacles.

Other suggestions have included deploying preplaced hardened field shelters near the central front for use in sheltering troops, equipment, headquarters and communications systems. (73) In addition the construction of similar artificial developments, for example reservoirs, as outlined by Cross, could be built with the defence in mind. Small obstacles could be created in peacetime (or near to a period of expected conflict) which could include minefields, concrete buildings and ditches. Finally, Keegan (74) has proposed the use of plastic piping buried 4-5 feet underground which could be filled, when necessary, with plastic explosive. When detonated, the effect would be a ditch wide enough to prevent tanks progressing further.
There have been two principal objections levelled against this form of barrier defence: firstly, there is a general reluctance to create a new Maginot Line and, secondly, there exists the political problem in that the FRG objects to a policy which would symbolize the permanent division of the two Germanys. It is possible, however, to refute such criticisms. Firstly, as Tillson (75) has argued, the Maginot Line was not fatally flawed. Rather, there were inadequate mobile reserves behind it. Tillson quotes Omar Bradley's comparison of French and German defences as further evidence (which is of particular importance in view of the earlier discussion of reserves): (76)

Although the German's fortified wall would not halt an intruder, it could slow down an attacking force while

Rommel called for reserves. Indeed, this was the intended function of his Atlantic wall. It was to blunt our assault and so split our forces that the enemy might find time to form his reserves and strike back in a counter attack. When used to screen a mobile reserve in this fashion, the concrete fortifications of a fixed defensive line can be worth many divisions. Without these mobile reserves, however, a fixed defensive line becomes useless. It was for this lack of mobile reserves that the Maginot Line became a trap for the French Army.

As to the second point regarding West German political objections to a barrier defence Tillson comments: (77)

Although ... (German) political considerations are real, the question of NATO's defensive capability should override them. It is difficult to see why defensive preparations would be more provocative than maintaining·standing forces oriented to the east. The de facto recognition of two Germanys has been granted implicitly in West Germany's Ostpolitik. Finally, if the Germans are serious about defending with minimum loss of territory and if defensive preparations are pursued with care over a period of years, the West German government should be able to overcome the objections of the border area residents.

Thus, a barrier defence would go some way towards creating a defensive deterrent strategy for the Western Alliance.

Increases in Prepositioned Supplies and War Stocks

An essential element in deterring a future. conflict is that sufficient stocks of fuel, equipment and replacements are seen to be readily available now, both for permanently deployed units and for US reinforcements flying into Europe. The position would have to be the same for defensive deterrence if it is to be credible. In the case of US reinforcements the UCS (78) believed that the US needed to complete its POMCUS (Prepositioned Material Configured to Unit Sets) programme. According to the UCS the programme is currently aimed at six division sets, plus support units in Europe (three in NORTHAG and three in CENTAG). At the time of the UCS study four sets have been placed and two were to be authorised. In the case of war stocks, and particularly ammunition, it has been argued that for NATO as a whole the aim should be for at least thirty days supply to be available with a longer-term aim of forty-five days.

A Note on Costs

Such a change in strategy to defensive deterrence would carry with it attendant economic costs which, although not as high as concepts and doctrines like FOFA and ALB would still entail a substantial input of additional finance. For example, the UCS (79) estimated that for the measures of fortifications, war stocks, increases in reserve forces and completion of the POMCUS programme, the cost would be under $100 billion over six years, or an annual real increase for NATO countries of two per cent per annum. The provision of light infantry forces would, however, be an additional cost to this. Kaufmann (80) has also provided a cost-estimate of transforming NATO's conventional forces. His estimate is reproduced as Figure 2.12. Here, for the most immediate steps to be taken, including the provision of a barrier defence, the cost would be (in billions of 1983 US dollars) $36.3 over six years.

Despite an increase in costs of this level a shift in NATO's strategy could also create substantial economies, not least in the savings which could be made from abandoning the nuclear role. In addition, as Chalmers (81) has argued, substantial savings could be made in ending NATO's out of area operations and capabilities and the procurement of over-sophisticated technology. The principal areas where expenditure could be reduced include weapons which have a deep attack role and offensive capability.

CONCLUSION

The conventional balance of forces is not as difficult for the West as has been standardly presented. Through a detailed threat assessment, it is possible to conclude that, on the central front, there exists a position of parity. Where there is an advantage held by the WP this is not near enough to guarantee victory in a conflict. Because of this it is possible to argue that NATO's reliance on flexible response is

Figure 2.12: Options for Strengthening the Land-based NATO forces in the Central Region of Europe

Billions of 1983 dollars

Option and force sustainability	Six-year cost	Cumulative six-year cost
First: 30 days		
Barriers	1.0	-
Improved line of communication	2.0	-
Collocated operating bases	0.3	-
War reserve stocks and training: 34 divisions. 15 days	24.1	-
War reserve stocks and training: 25 wings. 15 days	8.9	-
Total	36.3	36.3
Second: 30 days		
Three allied reserve divisions (a)	9.3	
War reserve stocks and training: 3 divisions. 30 days	4.3	
Total	13.6	49.9
Third: 30 days		
Five allied reserve divisions (b)	15.5	
War reserve stocks and training: 5 divisions. 30 days	7.1	
Five U.S. reserve divisions	20.6	
War reserve stocks and training: 5 divisions. 30 days	7.1	
Nine U.S. reserve wings of close air support	6.8	
War reserve stocks and training: 9 wings. 30 days	6.4	
Sealift for 8 U.S. divisions	15.4	
Total	78.9	128.8
Fourth: 45 days		
War reserve stocks and training: 47 divisions. 15 days	33.3	
War reserve stocks and training: 34 wings. 15 days	12.1	
Total	45.4	174.2

Fifth: indefinite		
U.S. conscription	72.0	
Seven allied wings of interceptor aircraft	14.1	
War reserve stocks and training: 7 wings. 45 days	7.4	
Total	93.5	267.7

(a) It is assumed that, of the 3 divisions, 2 come from West Germany and 1 from France.

(b) It is assumed that, of the 5 divisions, $\frac{2}{3}$ of a division comes from Britain, 3 from France and $1\frac{1}{3}$ from the Netherlands.

Source: Kaufmann, W.W., 'Nonnuclear Deterrence', in Steinbrunner, J.D. and L.V. Sigal (eds.), Alliance Security: NATO and the No-First Use Question, (The Brookings Institution, Washington, D.C., 1983), p.85.

unnecessary and that fundamental change could be made in the defence of the West. The most favourable method for this is the adoption of defensive deterrence and downgrading the nuclear role. This would not only lessen the possibilities of nuclear war, but would, ultimately, contribute towards solving the security dilemma in Europe.

NOTES AND REFERENCES

1. See No First Use, (Union of Concerned Scientists, Cambridge, Mass., 1983).

2. Lord Cameron et al., Diminishing the Nuclear Threat, (British Atlantic Committee, London, 1984).

3. See Strengthening Conventional Deterrence in Europe: The Report of the European Security Study, (Macmillan, London, 1983).

4. See Defence Without the Bomb, (Taylor and Francis, London, 1983); Without the Bomb, (Granada, 1985), and The Politics of Alternative Defence, (Granada, 1987).

5. See Evangelista, M.A., 'Stalin's Postwar Army Reappraised', International Security, vol. 7, no. 3, (Winter 1982/3), pp.110-38.

6. See, inter alia, ibid; Bracken, P., 'The NATO Defense Problem', Orbis, vol. 27, no. 1, (Spring 1983), pp.83-105; Chaney, O.P. 'The Soviet Threat to Europe: Prospects

for the 1980s', Parameters: Journal of the US Army War College, vol. 13, no. 3, (1983), pp.2-22; No First Use, op.cit.; Without the Bomb, op. cit.; Kaufmann, W.W., 'Nonnuclear Deterrence', in Steinbrunner, J.D. and L.V. Sigal, (eds), Alliance Security and the No-First-Use Question, (The Brookings Institution, Washington, D.C., 1983), pp.43-90; Krause, C., 'The Balance Between Conventional Forces in Europe', END Papers, 6, (Winter 1983-4), pp.41-59; Posen, B.R., 'Measuring the European Conventional Balance: Coping with Complexity in Threat Assessment', International Security, vol. 9, no. 3, (1984), pp.47-88; Mearsheimer, J.J., Conventional Deterrence, (Cornell University Press, 1983); Urban, M., 'Red Flag Over Germany', (three parts), Armed Forces, vol. 4, nos. 2, 3 and 4, (February, March, April, 1985), pp.69-74, 110-15, 149-55; Mako, W., US Ground Forces and the Defense of Central Europe, (The Brookings Institution, Washington, D.C., 1983); Meacham, J., 'The Sentry at the Gate: A Survey of NATO's Central Front', The Economist, (30th August 1986); Urban, M. and P. Pringle, 'Assessing the Arms Divide', The Independent, (7th May 1987).

7.   Mearsheimer, op. cit., p.169.

8.   Quoted in Hiatt, F., 'Does Pentagon Know Best About the Soviet Threat?', Washington Post, (2nd April 1986), p.21.

9.   See Soviet Military Power, (US Department of Defense, annually).

10.   Posen, op. cit., p.51.

11.   Ibid., p.53.

12.   The Military Balance 1986-1987, (International Institute for Strategic Studies, London, 1986). There are, however, considerable problems with using this publication. See my paper Critiques of the IISS Military Balance, (Defence Information Groups, Manchester, 1984), and the references there.

13.   Ibid., p.225.

14.   See Mearsheimer, Conventional Deterrence, op. cit., p.168. Mearsheimer uses official US Congressional Budget Office (CBO) Studies which quote the ADEs figure listed later in the section. In particular he is using Hillier, P., Strengthening NATO: POMCUS and Other Approaches, (CBO, Washington D.C., 1979), pp.53-7 and Hillier, P. and N. Slatkin, US Ground Forces: Design and Cost Alternatives for NATO and Non-NATO Contingencies, (CBO, Washington D.C., December 1980), pp.23-4. The use of the ADEs

measure has been criticised by the British Government in a section, 'Calculating the Conventional Balance', in vol. 1, Statement on the Defence Estimates, 1987 (Her Majesty's Stationery Office, London, 1987), p.61. The argument being that it introduces an element of subjectivity into the process of threat assessment. Whilst this is undoubtedly true it remains the case that the ADEs measure is more preferable as it accounts for the technological advantages held by the West which the traditional 'bean count' ignores.

15.　Cordesman, A.H., 'The NATO Central Region and the Balance of Uncertainty', Armed Forces Journal International, (July 1983), pp.18-58. Reprinted in Current News, No. 1034, (3rd August 1983). References in this paper refer to the latter edition.

16.　Mako, op. cit.

17.　Cordesman, op. cit., p.3.

18.　Ibid., p.10.

19.　Kaufmann, op. cit., p.55.

20.　Mako, op. cit.

21.　Ibid., p.43. Much of what follows is taken from Mako, pp.45-8.

22.　Cordesman, op. cit., p.4.

23.　Statement on the Defence Estimates, 1987, op. cit.

24.　See Hansard, Columns 263-4, written answers, (17th May 1985).

25.　Carnegie Panel on US Security, Challenges for US National Security, Part II, Assessing the Balance: Defense Spending and Conventional Forces, (Carnegie Endowment for International Peace, Washington D.C., 1981), p.71.

26.　See Epstein, J.M., Measuring Military Power: The Soviet Air Threat to Europe, (Taylor and Francis, London, 1984), 280pp.

27.　NATO and the Warsaw Pact: Force Comparisons, (NATO, Brussels, 1984).

28.　Cordesman, op. cit., p.35.

29.　Ibid., p.5.

30.　The best recent account of Soviet naval forces and strategy is Ranft, B. and G. Till, The Sea in Soviet Strategy, (Macmillan, London, 1983), 240pp.

31.　See 'Heritage says Soviets Hold Conventional Forces Lead', Washington Times, (5th March 1986), p.8B.

32.　Carnegie Panel, op. cit., pp.120, 122.

33.　Kaufmann, op. cit., p.49.

34.　Mearsheimer, Conventional Deterrence, op. cit.

35. Ibid., chapter six.

36. Ibid., p.168.

37. Martin, L., Before the Day After: Can NATO Defend Europe?, (Newnes Books, Middlesex, 1985), p.43.

38. Mearsheimer, op. cit., pp.174-5.

39. Ibid. Mearsheimer comments, p. 47: 'A related phenomenon compounds the attacker's problem in piercing the defender's front. Although the attacker may have a significant advantage in the number of forces available for the crucial breakthrough battles, the attacker will undoubtedly not be able to line up all of his forces along the front; there will simply not be enough room for all of them. A portion will have to be placed in rear echelons, behind the forces that directly engage the defender. Located behind the front they will have little direct impact on the battle, so that the defender will be in the enviable position of being able to combat the attacker's forces piecemeal. This bonus is analogous to the crossing-the-T phenomenon known in naval warfare'.

40. Wicker, T., 'The Other Balance (1)', New York Times, (9th April 1982), p.27.

41. See, inter alia., Nelson, D.N. (ed.), Soviet Allies: The Warsaw Pact and the Issue of Reliability, (Westview Press, Boulder, Colorado, 1984), 273pp; The Threat: Inside the Soviet Military Machine, (rev. ed., New English Library, London, 1985); Ned Lebow, R., 'The Soviet Offensive in Europe: the Schlieffen Plan Revisited?', International Security, vol. 9, no. 4, (Spring 1985), pp.44-78; Johnson, R., et al., 'The Armies of the Warsaw Pact Northern Tier', Survival, vol. 23, no. 4, (July/August 1981), pp.174-82; Herspring, D.R. and I. Volgyes, 'How Reliable are Eastern European Armies?', Survival, vol. 22, no. 5, (September/October 1980), pp.208-18. For a contrary argument to the view that the Soviet and East European Armies are plagued with difficulties see Luttwak, E.N., 'Delusions of Soviet Weakness', Commentary, (January 1985), pp.32-8.

42. See Chapter 1, 'The Soviet Need to Defeat NATO Quickly' in Vigor, P.H., Soviet Blitzkrieg Theory, (Macmillan, London, 1983), pp.1-9 for elaboration on this point.

43. See Rogers, Gen. B.W., 'Follow-On Forces Attack (FOFA): Myths and Realities', NATO Review, vol. 32, no. 6, (December 1984), p.7.

44. See Weinberger, C., 'Improving NATO's Conven-

tional Capabilities', Nelson, <u>A Report to the United States Congress</u>, (June 1984).

45.   See Greenwood, D., 'Strengthening Conventional Deterrence: Doctrine, New Technology and Resources', <u>NATO Review</u>, vol. 32, no. 4, (August 1984), p.9. It is of considerable interest to note that, in the subsequent issue of <u>NATO Review</u>, General Rogers (article referenced in Note 43 above) claims that Chris Donnelly (whose research Greenwood relied on for his contribution) is in full support of FOFA. Donnelly also contributes a paper to the same issue on 'The Soviet Concept of Echeloning'.

46.   Weinberger, <u>op. cit.</u>

47.   Greenwood, D., 'Economic Implications: Finding the Resources for an Effective Conventional Defence', in Windass, S., (ed.), <u>Avoiding Nuclear War: Common Security as a Strategy for the Defence of the West</u>, (Brassey's Defence Publishers, London, 1985), p.79.

48.   See <u>Defence Commitments and Resources and the Defence Estimates 1985-6, Third Report from the Defence Committee, Session 1984-85</u>, vol. 1, (Her Majesty's Stationery Office, London, 1985).

49.   For a detailed critique of FOFA/Deep Strike highlighting the problems of preemption see Evangelista, M.A., 'Offense or Defense: A Tale of Two Commissions', <u>World Policy Journal</u>, vol. 1, no. 1, (1982), pp.445-69.

50.   See Berg, P. and G. Herolf, '"Deep Strike": New Technologies for Conventional Interdiction', in <u>The Arms Race and Arms Control</u>, (SIPRI/Taylor and Francis, London, 1984), pp.126-53 for a detailed discussion of possible Soviet countermeasures.

51.   Ned Lebow, <u>op. cit.</u>, p.78.

52.   A useful overview of the available literature, together with a comprehensive bibliography, is contained in Brauch, H.G. and L. Unterseher, 'Getting Rid of Nuclear Weapons: A Review of a Few Proposals for a Conventional Defense of Europe', <u>Journal of Peace Research</u>, vol. 21, no. 2, (1984), pp.193-205. See also ADC, <u>op. cit.</u>; Clarke, M., 'The Alternative Defence Debate: Non-Nuclear Defence Policies for Europe', <u>ADIU Occasional Papers</u>, no. 3, (Armament and Disarmament Information Unit, University of Sussex, 1985); Johansen, R.C., 'Toward an Alternative Security System', <u>World Policy Paper</u>, no. 24, (World Policy Institute, New York, 1983); Tatchell, P., <u>Democratic Defence: A Non-Nuclear Alternative</u>, (GMP, London, 1985).

53.   See <u>Without the Bomb</u>, <u>op. cit.</u>

54.   See pages 49-52 in Booth, K., 'The Case for Non-Nuclear Defence', in Roper, J. (ed.), The Future of British Defence Policy, (Gower, Aldershot, 1985), pp.32-56. See also Does the Danger of "Nuclear Blackmail" Necessitate a World of Nuclear-Weapon States?, (Defence Information Groups, Manchester, 1986), 12pp.
55.   Booth, op. cit.
56.   Tillson, J.C.F, 'The Forward Defense of Europe', Military Review, vol. LXI, no. 5, (May 1981), pp.66-76.
57.   Canby, S.L., 'Solving the Defense Riddle', New Republic, vol. 182, no. 17, (26th April 1980), pp.20-3.
58.   Mako, op. cit., p.89.
59.   Martin, L., op. cit.
60.   Ibid., p.54.
61.   Hamilton, A.H., 'Redressing the Conventional Balance: NATO's Reserve Military Manpower', International Security, vol. 10, no. 1, (Summer 1985), pp.111-36.
62.   Ibid., p.111.
63.   Canby, S.L., 'The Alliance and Europe: Part IV, Military Doctrine and Technology', Adelphi Papers, no. 109, (IISS, London, 1975). This paper goes into some detail as to the possible use of reserve forces.
64.   Canby, S.L., 'Military Reform and the Art of War', International Security Review, vol. 7, no. 3, (Fall 1982), pp.245-68.
65.   Loser, J., 'The Security Policy Options for Non-Communist Europe', Armada International, no. 2, (1982), pp.66-75.
66.   See Cordesman, op. cit., p.5.
67.   Canby, S. and I. Dorfer, 'More Troops, Fewer Missiles', Foreign Policy, no. 53, (Winter 1983-4), p.12.
68.   Keegan, J., quoted in No First Use, op. cit., p.28.
69.   Kaufmann, 'Nonnuclear Deterrence', op. cit.
70.   Freeman, W.D. Jnr., 'NATO Central Region Forward Defense: Correcting the Strategy/Force Mismatch', National Defense University National Security Affairs Issue Paper, No. 81-3, (1981), pp.11-12.
71.   Cross, Maj. T., 'Forward Defence - A Time for Change?', RUSI Journal of the Royal United Services Institute for Defence Studies, vol. 130, no. 2, (June 1985), pp.19-24.
72.   Ibid., p.22.
73.   One of the principal advocates of preplaced hardened field defences is Major J.B.A. Bailey. See his 'The Case for Preplaced Hardened Field Defenses', International

Defense Review, no. 7, (1984), pp.887-92 and 'Preplaced Hardened Field Defences', British Army Review, no. 72, (August 1982), pp.26-30.

74. See his letter 'Merits of Fixed Defence', The Times, (30th October 1984). See also 'Europe's Pipe Mines - Prospects and Problems', Jane's Defence Weekly, (22nd September 1984).

75. Tillson, op. cit.

76. Bradley, O., quoted in Ibid., p.68.

77 Ibid., p.69. See, however, Drozdiak, W., 'W. Germans Disavow Role for "Pipe" Bomb Along East Border', Washington Post, (24th August 1984), p.25.

78. See No First Use, op. cit., p.34.

79. Ibid., pp.34-5.

80. See Kaufmann, op. cit., pp.79-90.

81. See Chalmers, M., 'Can NATO Afford a Non-Suicidal Strategy?', in Prins, G., (ed.), The Choice: Nuclear Weapons Versus Security, (Chatto and Windus, London, 1984), pp.218-23 and 'Paying for a Real Defence', in Chalmers, M., Paying for Defence, (Pluto Press, London, 1985), pp.158-73.

Chapter Three

NEW CONVENTIONAL TECHNOLOGY AND ALTERNATIVE DEFENCE: HELP OR HINDRANCE?

Philip Gummett

INTRODUCTION

New technology is sometimes invoked as a panacea for the problems faced by non-nuclear defence policies. While it undoubtedly has much to offer, there are also dangers, of political, economic, strategic and operational types, which we must take into account.

The background to current interest in new conventional technologies is concern about the adequacy of the existing nuclear and conventional defences of Western Europe. Yet such concerns are not new. (1) In the 1950s, the doctrine of massive retaliation was introduced to cover, amongst other things, the extension of the United States' deterrent capability to include the defence of Europe. As the credibility of massive retaliation declined in the face of increasing Soviet nuclear capacity (particularly its capacity to strike directly at the United States), moves began to replace massive retaliation with what eventually became the doctrine of flexible response. However, a key element of the new strategy, namely the build up of conventional forces, was not in the event achieved. This raised doubts about the credibility of flexible response, and by the 1970s these doubts had extended to include the credibility of the United States nuclear guarantee to Europe and the coupling of United States strategic forces to the European theatre. The outcome of this debate was the 1979 decision to introduce cruise and Pershing II missiles into Europe in what, as it turned out, was a misplaced attempt to reassure public opinion on this score.

Public reaction to this decision, coupled with

developments in technology, provide the context for the recent re-thinking of NATO doctrine and have led, amongst other things, to the development of some new 'Deep Strike' military doctrines. (2) One of these, called Air Land Battle, was developed by the United States Army to provide it with the means of fighting a highly mobile war in any part of the world, including Western Europe. Among the relevant features of this doctrine are its emphasis upon the integration of chemical and nuclear weapons into the battle, and upon launching offensive manoeuvres behind enemy lines. Because the focus of this chapter is on non-nuclear defence, no discussion is offered of Air Land Battle, although it is criticised elsewhere in this book. The other major new doctrine, called Follow-On Forces Attack, emerged from the headquarters of the Supreme Allied Commander Europe (SACEUR). Its central feature is the combination of forward defence against the attacking Soviet forces and longer range attacks upon follow-on forces as they make their way up to the front. It is also concerned with strikes against such crucial enemy targets as airfields and choke points along the supply and communications lines. In a sense, it has long been NATO policy to make deep strikes against crucial targets, but the technologies that are becoming available today enable this doctrine to be implemented in a much more dramatic way than had previously been possible with conventional weapons.

In this chapter, we examine the nature of the new technology and some of the issues which it raises. Among these are its costs (both direct financial costs and opportunity costs), and various problems that may impede its adoption on military or international relations grounds. Finally, we consider the use of the new technologies in the context of a non-provocative, purely <u>defensive</u> defence policy.

THE NEW TECHNOLOGY

Developments in microelectronics, sensors, and new materials have opened up a vista of new conventional weapons with capacities such as have only been dreamed of before. The possibility now exists of real-time long-range 'acquisition', tracking and targeting of fixed and mobile targets through the use of long-range sideways-looking radar borne in an aircraft which patrols parallel to the line of conflict while remaining well behind friendly lines. Sophisticated data processing and communications links will transmit this information to commanders in various parts of the battlefield. New sensors offer the prospect of warheads behaving in 'smart' or even 'brilliant' fashion by, for example, following a laserbeam to a target, or by distinguishing a tank from a jeep and homing in on it. New conventional warheads allow more efficient use of explosive charges which, coupled with high accuracy of delivery, may allow substitution for nuclear warheads in certain roles. New materials allow aircraft and remotely piloted vehicles to operate under even more extreme conditions and, through the use of so-called stealth technology, to experience reduced risk of detection. The whole battlefield is in the process of becoming much more highly co-ordinated through advanced data and communication links. (3) The overall effect could be to introduce a qualitative change in the nature of warfare.

As an example, consider the Multiple Launch Rocket System (MLRS). Phase one of this system, which is already in use in some NATO armies, allows twelve rockets to be fired in the space of one minute over a range of about thirty kilometres, a rate of fire which could previously only have been achieved through the use of three artillery battalions. The resulting devastation would extend over an area roughly equal to six soccer fields. Phase two involves a more advanced warhead, and phase three will involve terminally guided submunitions. An example of these is the SKEET system. (4) A SKEET submunition weighs 2.7 kg and twenty-four can be fitted per missile. It is intended to be fired over a tank column, where it will drop on a parachute, wobbling slightly as it falls and thereby being able to scan an area of ground 50 x 100 metres in area. It will use infra-red detectors to find the characteristic heat signature of its target, such as a tank, and when within a range of 10 to 30 metres from the target it will detonate a small 500g warhead which will forge an armour-piercing projectile. If it fails to find a target of the designated type the warhead detonates by an alternative procedure to produce metallic fragments which would be lethal to personnel or thin-skinned vehicles. One salvo of missiles loaded with the SKEET submunition is thought to be capable of destroying a company of tanks.

SKEET, or other advanced munitions, could of course be fitted into larger and longer-range air-to-ground or ground-to-ground rockets. NATO countries are already collab-orating on the specification for a long range stand-off missile which might be a cruise or a ballistic missile to be fired from an aircraft at a distant target. There is also interest in the use of the Pershing II or even some stages of the Trident missile for the ground-to-ground missiles. New runway-destroying weapons such as the British JP-233 system, which both craters the airfield and scatters mines to impede runway clearance, are also now available. In addition, work is proceeding on advanced anti-tank weapons which would have true 'fire and forget' capabilities. Most current anti-tank weapons require the operator to maintain some sort of visual contact with the target during the flight time of the missile; this may be difficult in practice because of the nature of the terrain or because of enemy fire.

The advantages of these new technologies are readily apparent. They can be summed up in the expression 'force multiplication'. (5) This term is intended to imply that, by the use of these new technologies, an existing military force can multiply its effectiveness. This may, for example, allow a reduced number of sorties for the destruction of certain kinds of targets. For example, if the object were to destroy 60% of a Soviet division, comprising 3,000 vehicles, of which one third would be armoured, then the number of successful sorties required using free falling 250kg iron bombs has been estimated to be 2,200. Using free fall submunitions the number would drop to 300, and using terminally guided submunitions to 50 or 60. (6) Greater accuracy and lethality, better penetration of enemy territory, and better command, control, communications and intelligence are among the other attractions offered by the new technologies.

NATO is now committed to exploratory development of many of these new technologies. Following an initiative taken by the American Secretary of Defence, Mr Weinberger, in June 1982, studies are under way within NATO on the evaluation of options and on multi-national participation in the development and production of what have come to be called collectively the 'emerging technologies' (ET). (7)

COSTS OF THE NEW TECHNOLOGIES

It is far from clear what these new technologies would cost. Most of them are, at present, little more than 'brochure promises'. Moreover, any estimates that are cited must be viewed in the context of an inflation rate for military equipment which is higher than the inflation rate for economies as a whole; within that, cost escalation on advanced equipment tends to be greater still.

One estimate, by Wikner, suggests that a substantial package of new conventional technologies could be purchased for an expenditure of $1.3b per year over a period of ten years. (8) The package could comprise, for NATO's central region, 1,100 conventionally armed Pershing IIs, 15,000 anti-armour helicopter-borne submunitions, and 30 aircraft per corps and 2,000 stand-off weapons, and surveillance and targeting equipment, amongst other things. The US share of this expenditure would be some $350m per year which, notes Wikner, (9) is less than the United States currently spends per year on ammunition for training. Other estimates provide similar figures. One, for example, cites a total cost of $10b to $30b spread over ten years, while General Rogers (SACEUR) suggests that NATO could be substantially re-equipped at the cost of a sustained additional 4% per annum in real terms, over current defence budgets, throughout the 1980s. (10)

To the immediate financial costs, however, should be added the opportunity costs of this investment, and at least two are worth comment. First there is an argument within NATO circles that investment in research, development and production of the emerging technologies might be made at the price of diverting resources from more immediate needs upon which the readiness of NATO forces, and their capacity to sustain a war, might depend. Thus reference has been made to the need for aircraft shelters, fuel, ammunition, chemical and biological warfare suits, and training. Decisions taken in late 1984 by NATO ministers to improve ammunition stocks, shelters, and other items no doubt offered some consolation to advocates of this position. (11)

The other opportunity cost which should be mentioned here arises from the heavy demands upon computing, microelectronic, and software skills which the emerging defence technologies make. Taylor (12) has noted that if we take a ten year period centred on 1984, and make some conservative estimates about the rate of computerisation of military systems, then we see:

the number of computers deployed in battle systems

will increase by 50 to 100 times; the amount of store per computer will increase by 10 - 100 times, from tens of kilobytes to tens of megabytes; data transmission will increase by 10 - 100 times; the data-base storage capacity will increase from almost nothing to hundreds of megabytes.

He goes on to note that the amount of software deployed in battle systems will go up by 1,000 - 10,000 times and that the value of this software and associated data bases will go up by very much more than this as the people involved in producing and maintaining them get more scarce and expensive. Hence, if it is the case, as is often argued, that there already exists in Western economies a shortage of skilled personnel in these fields, it may be worth reflecting upon the implications of further demands arising from the military sector. National security is a complex concept: it depends upon economic as well as military strength, and so a nation that buys its military strength at the expense of its economic base cannot in the long-run be truly secure.

PROBLEMS OF ADOPTION OF NEW TECHNOLOGY

Assuming that the resources can be found, what obstacles lie in the way of the adoption of these new technologies, and what problems do the technologies themselves generate? I list below eight issues which require further examination. The first four are of a military nature; the fifth, sixth and seventh are problems in international relations; and the last concerns the feasibility of using the new technologies within a genuinely defensive framework.

First, we may question how enthusiastic the military is about ET. There are precedents for new technology not being received with heartfelt enthusiasm in military circles. One is reminded of the remarks made by Field Marshal Earl Haig, in 1925, when he said: (13)

I'm all for using aeroplanes and tanks, but they are only accessories to the man and the horse, and I feel sure that as time goes on you will find just as much use for the horse - the well-bred horse - as you have ever done in the past.

It may be unfair to raise that as an analogy, but it is

certainly fair to note the inconsistency which appears to exist between, for example, the expressed enthusiasm of the United States Army for the Air Land Battle doctrine, and the priority given to the M-1 tank, the infantry carrier, and the attack helicopter over the ET programme in the US Army's equipment modernisation programme. (14) It is likely that resistance to the new technologies will be in rough proportion to their impact upon organisational patterns and existing tactical procedures, as well as to their impact upon other elements of the military budget. There are also more 'objective' reasons for military doubts, as our next three concerns show.

Second, the adoption of the new technologies is complicated by the current diversity of military doctrines within NATO. In particular, the requirements of Air Land Battle and of Follow-On Forces Attack seem, to the outside observer, far from identical, and this cannot help in the specification of operational requirements for new equipment on a NATO-wide basis.

Third, we may wonder what would happen if the elaborate systems upon which these new technologies depend broke down. It is clear that among the most vulnerable elements of these systems will be the airborne surveillance systems, and if these could be attacked, or even simply jammed, then surely the efficiency of the system as a whole would be gravely impaired. If commanders in the field had been trained to operate in a way that depended upon externally-supplied information, and had got used, for example, to map reading systems which were electronic and which showed on a display unit the location of friendly and enemy forces, how would they cope when those aids to decision-making suddenly ceased to be available?

This leads to a fourth concern, which is that of enemy ·counter-measures. Military technology does not stand still. The lowest level of counter-measure may be illustrated by a procedure used by Israeli tank commanders during the 1973 Middle Eastern war. When finding themselves targeted by a precision guided munition, the Israelis learnt to stop the tank, allow the missile to approach and then lurch forward at the last moment. The missile's reaction time was unable to cope with such a rapid manoeuvre. (15) But many more sophisticated types of counter-measures are available. First, and given that there is evidence to the effect that interdiction attacks, of the type which the Deep Strike approaches exemplify, work best under conditions of air superiority, (16) one could expect the Warsaw Pact to respond by massive air strikes against NATO air-bases and missile launching positions. Perhaps, too, they could develop some of the new target acquisition and tracking devices to the point where they would be able to counter anti-tank guided weapons at points where they were concentrated, such as, for example, when being transported in lightly armoured vehicles to, or around, the battlefield. They might also engage in various kinds of electronic warfare, and here it is appropriate to note that experts are concerned that NATO's current use of the new technologies is somewhat indiscriminate in terms of the volume of signals being transmitted at any given moment. In the shorthand of the technicians, current ET 'shouts', and concern is being expressed that systems should be developed which 'whisper' instead. The Warsaw Pact may also develop anti-ballistic missile point defences for use against attacking NATO missiles. It might also engage in some simple tactical changes. If, for example, NATO strategy became predicated on the assumption that it could hold the first echelon of a Warsaw Pact attack but needed to destroy the second echelon before it reached the battle area, then one obvious response would be to increase the size of the first echelon attack; another would be to speed up the transit of the second echelon. Current debate about whether Soviet doctrine really does depend upon the assembly of forces into echelons, or whether it relies more heavily than some have conceded upon fast moving and relatively self-contained operational manoeuvre groups (OMG) casts further doubt upon the wisdom of NATO putting too many eggs into the Deep Strike basket. (17)

A fifth issue is whether NATO can afford to develop the emerging technologies without substantially more international collaboration in research, development and production than has been the case in the recent past. Concern was initially expressed that the 1982 ET initiative was in essence a Pentagon marketing ploy designed to swamp Europe with American-produced defence systems. Had this been so, it would have represented a grave threat to the defence industries of Europe, and also to some of the related civilian industries. Leaving this point aside, however, it must also be admitted that the record on collaboration is patchy to say the least. In the missile field alone, it has been reported that 11 firms in seven NATO countries are working on anti-tank guided weapons; 18 firms in seven countries on ground to air weapons; ten firms in seven countries on air-to-ground weapons; and so on. A new political emphasis was put upon collaboration in defence research, development and production by the former British Secretary of State for Defence, Mr Heseltine, and one of the fruits of his initiative was the agreement in May 1984 on collaboration in certain of the new technologies. But it is still early days, the sums at stake are presently not great, and it remains to be seen whether, as the commercial stakes rise, the production of these new systems generates more alliance tension than harmony. (18)

A sixth area of concern is that of arms control. The introduction into Europe of conventionally-armed Pershing-II missiles, ground-launched cruise missiles, or any other systems that have in the past been used only in nuclear roles, raises serious difficulties for the negotiation of arms control agreements because of the problems associated with verification of any such agreements. (19) Some sources refer to the need to develop functionally related observable differences (FRODS) between nuclear and conventionally-armed delivery systems, but it is far from clear what these might be. Some refer to the possibilities of specific radar signatures; others to different physical base layouts; others to characteristic operating procedures; and yet others (20) to the argument that there is apparently a small difference in the trajectory followed by conventionally, as distinct from nuclear, armed missiles.

A seventh problem is that of crisis stability. There is a danger that in avoiding the need for early use of nuclear weapons NATO may find itself in the position of having to make early use of Deep Strike conventional weapons. One can only guess what the Soviet response might be. We may wonder, first, whether they would take the trouble to wait and see what type of munition was carried by, let us say, a Pershing missile before deciding how to respond, or whether they would accept that the use of area dispersal submunitions at a time when, perhaps, the Soviet Union was unable to reply in kind, merited a nuclear response. One may also wonder in this respect how good the NATO decision making machinery would be for maintaining political control over decisions to undertake deep strikes. To the extent that it is a fair analogy, British experience over the decision to sink the Argentine battleship General Belgrano is not encouraging. A further feature of the crisis stability issue concerns the deterrent value of 'force multipliers'. The question here, in essence, is: <u>do force multipliers deter as well as force does?</u> In other words, is the deterrent value of sophisticated technology, much of the capacity of which may not be directly obvious, as great as that of forces which are clearly visible on the ground? Without doubt, NATO would have to take care to ensure that the capabilities of its equipment were well understood by its potential adversary.

Finally, what are the prospects for using the new conventional technologies in a purely defensive, non-provocative way? Much more thinking must be done on this subject, not least by those, such as the Labour Party, who advocate movement towards such a defence policy. It is necessary to consider such questions as:

(a) What is to be done if NATO territory is captured?
(b) Would NATO need an offensive capability in order to regain lost ground, and if so, how would it ensure that that capacity was limited in scope?
(c) How long could NATO forces survive on the battlefield if subjected to constant Warsaw Pact air attack?
(d) If, following from (c), there is merit in having the capacity to destroy Warsaw Pact airfields, how would its use be circumscribed?
(e) How much of the so-called defensive technology which NATO might acquire could be used in an offensive mode?

Clearly, the distinction between defensive and offensive weaponry is not one of technology alone but is also one of force numbers, patterns of organisation, and training, and it is only in that overall context that relatively unambiguous signals about NATO's capacity and intentions could be sent to the Eastern bloc countries.

While there may be considerable political resistance to the introduction of much of the technology associated with Deep Strike doctrines, because of understandable concern about the provocative aspects of these doctrines, there may nevertheless be much that can be extracted from these approaches for use in the shorter range defensive battle. Better surveillance, command and control, submunitions, and guidance systems all have great potential as force multipliers. If they can be developed and deployed in weapons which are so configured, and whose users have been so trained, that they could be used for only extremely limited offensive manoeuvres, then they may well in the end add considerably to the overall security of Europe. The danger that must be avoided is the development of technically feasible weapons systems in isolation from clear conceptions of the purposes for which they are required. Nor should wide-ranging weapons development programmes in the ET field (and, a fortiori, in the Strategic Defense Initiative field) be justified on the grounds that the technical advances which will probably result will have widespread uses in defence technology. There are cheaper and less dangerous ways of obtaining such benefits. They depend, however, upon hard, clear thought and a willingness by political authorities to involve themselves in the weapons development process to the point where they can be sure that the process is directed towards the equipment needs of politically acceptable military doctrines.

NOTES AND REFERENCES

1.   For an excellent historical review, see Lawrence Freedman, The Evolution of Nuclear Strategy, (London: Macmillan, 1981), chapter 19.
2.   These are reviewed in Boyd D. Sutton et al., 'Deep Attack Concepts and the Defence of Central Europe', Survival, vol. xxvi, no. 2, March/April 1984, pp.50-70; Hew Strachan, 'Conventional Defence in Europe', International Affairs, vol. 61, no. 1, Winter 1984/85, pp.27-43; Per Berg and Gunilla Herolf, '"Deep Strike": new technologies for conventional interdiction', in Stockholm International Peace Research Institutue, The Arms Race and Arms Control 1984 (London: Taylor and Francis, 1984); and General Bernard W. Rogers, 'Follow-on Forces Attack (FOFA): Myths and Realities', NATO Review, vol. 32, no. 6, December 1984, pp.1-9.
3.   For further details of the new technologies see Berg and Herolf, op. cit.; The Economist Intelligence Unit, Defence Papers: A Transatlantic Debate over Emerging Technologies and Defence Capabilities (London: The Economist, Special Report, no. 172, 1984); International Institute for Strategic Studies, Strategic Survey 1983-4, (London: IISS, 1984), pp. 12-17; and much of Seymour J. Deitchman, Military Power and the Advance of Technology, (Boulder, Colorado: Westview Press, 1983).
4.   See Fred Wikner, 'Soviet Strategy and the Role of Conventional Forces', in Economist Intelligence Unit, op.

cit., pp.17-18.

5. See British Atlantic Committee, Diminishing the Nuclear Threat: NATO's Defence and New Technology, (London: British Atlantic Committee, 1984).

6. Wikner, loc. cit., p.16.

7. IISS, op. cit., p.16; and North Atlantic Assembly, Military Committee, Draft Interim Report of the Sub-Committee on Conventional Defence in Europe, Rapporteur Mr Karsten Voigt (Brussels: NAA, MC/CD (84) 1, 1984), pp.16-17.

8. Wikner, loc. cit., pp.19-21.

9. European Security Study Group (ESECS), Strengthening Conventional Deterrence in Europe: Proposals for the 1980s (London: Macmillan, 1983).

10. Cited in Phil Williams and William Wallace, 'Emerging Technologies and European Security', Survival, vol. xxvi, no. 2, March/April 1984, p.72.

11. The Guardian, 21 November 1984.

12. John M. Taylor, 'Computing and Software' in Economist Intelligence Unit, op. cit., p.61.

13. Cited in David Divine, The Blunted Sword, (London: Hutchinson, 1964), p.147.

14. Cited in Williams and Wallace, op. cit., p.73.

15. Lance S. Davidson, 'The Impact of Precision-Guided Munitions on War', Royal United Services Institute and Brassey's Defence Yearbook (London: Brassey's, 1984), p.247.

16. See Berg and Herolf, op. cit., p.139-40.

17. For discussion of the significance of OMGs, see Rogers, op. cit., and the article by Christopher Donnelly, 'The Development of the Soviet Concept of Echeloning', in the same issue of NATO Review. For further more general discussion of countermeasures, see Boyd et. al., op. cit.; Wallace and Williams, op. cit.; and Berg and Herolf, op. cit.

18. For further argument on this theme, see Judith Reppy and Philip Gummett, 'Economic and Technical Cooperation', in Catherine M. Kelleher and Gale A. Mattox (eds), Evolving European Defence Policies, (Lexington, Mass.: Lexington Books, 1987).

19. See British Atlantic Committee, op. cit., pp.24-5.

20. Wikner, cited in Strachan, op. cit., p.38.

Chapter Four

THE EVOLUTION OF LABOUR'S DEFENCE AND SECURITY POLICY

Mike Gapes

INTRODUCTION

The June 1983 General Election was a disaster for the Labour Party. One of the issues on which Labour lost support was undoubtedly defence. Internal divisions in the Party between 1980 and 1983; a failure properly to present its policy prior to the election; and public disagreements on defence policy during the campaign itself, all seriously damaged the credibility of Labour as the alternative party of government.

Although the electorate knew what we were against, (cruise, Trident, nuclear weapons in general), they did not know what we were positively for. That was hardly surprising, for nor did the Labour Party itself! Labour's opponents were therefore able to get away with distortion and misrepresentation of its policy and were able successfully to imply that it would somehow leave the country 'defenceless'.

Part of the problem was that a study group set up in 1981 had not completed its work at the time Mrs Thatcher called the 1983 General Election, one year early. The study group had just begun consideration of the first draft of its final report at the end of April, when Mrs Thatcher decided to cash in on her Falklands legacy and on Labour's obvious internal divisions on a variety of policy areas. Major defence policy issues remained unresolved. The National Executive Committee had naively assumed that the election would not be held until the end of Mrs Thatcher's five year term. Thus at the time the election was called there were a host of policy committees still beavering away developing new policy statements to be put to the September 1983 Annual Party Conference. Defence was no exception. The draft report could not be published.

Even worse, the Campaign Document which became the Manifesto, 'The New Hope for Britain', was ambiguous on key points and therefore open to differing and damaging interpretations, e.g. on whether we would scrap Polaris regardless of what happened in negotiations or whether Labour would keep it if the negotiations failed; and on how a commitment to cut defence spending significantly could be reconciled with a commitment to a strong conventional defence. Michael Heseltine's disinformation unit in the Ministry of Defence was easily able to set the terms of debate as being Labour's divisions and its weakness in the face of an alleged massive Soviet threat. The Liberals and Social Democrats assisted the process, by concentrating their attacks on Labour for its 'unilateralism' and only talking about 'dual-key' control arrangements on cruise missiles rather than opposition to their deployment.

The Campaign for Nuclear Disarmament had made a big impact in the years prior to the election, but election law and its own status as a broad mass movement and pressure group prevented it having any significant impact during the election campaign itself. By its very nature CND was an anti-nuclear campaign. It could not endorse a specific non-nuclear defence policy. That was the job of the opposition parties. But in 1983 they totally failed to move the debate onto the government's own dangerous and expensive nuclear escalatory policy.

After June 1983 it was generally recognised throughout the Labour Party that a new start was required. A model motion sponsored by the umbrella group, the Labour Disarmament Liaison Committee, was widely circulated and reached the agenda of the Autumn 1983 Annual Conference of the Party in Brighton where it was adopted with strong support. It instructed the National Executive Committee to produce 'a credible, comprehensive and effective non-nuclear defence policy' that would enhance the security of the people of Britain.

The new National Executive Committee and new Party leadership quickly acted upon this resolution. A Joint Working Party of eight members of the Parliamentary Labour Party, eight members of the National Executive Committee and six co-opted specialists was set up.

The Joint Policy Committee format was an innovation

which was subsequently applied to all the other policy making committees of the Kinnock era. In the past study groups and policy committees had often been dominated by members of the National Executive Committee, co-opted backbench Members of Parliament, and academic advisers. Their membership had been large and unwieldy and there had been a tendency for the policy to be developed without serious involvement of the senior front bench members of Parliament who would have to implement the policy in government. The new procedure was designed to lead to the development of one cohesive policy rather than two or more conflicting policies, and the front bench and shadow cabinet role was therefore to be considerably enhanced in this process.

After six months detailed discussion of numerous drafts by the Joint Policy Committee - which represented a very broad spectrum of opinion, ranging from Lord Gregson (of the Defence Manufacturers Association) and Pat Duffy M.P. on the right to National Executive Members Eric Heffer and Jo Richardson on the left - a 20,000 word report was produced.

Although the total membership of the Joint Policy Committee was some twenty individuals, the key work of resolving difficult areas was done by a smaller sub-group of half a dozen which met regularly between meetings of the full committee. It included the deputy defence spokesperson, Denzil Davies M.P., the deputy foreign affairs spokesperson George Robertson M.P., and two of the co-opted academic advisers. All detailed drafting was done by the secretary, Mike Gapes, and he and Denzil Davies were given authority to finalise the text and reconcile any inconsistencies. Their final version of the report was then submitted to the International Committee of the Party and then considered by the full National Executive Committee.

At the NEC Roy Hattersley the Deputy Leader moved, and Neil Kinnock the Leader seconded, the adoption of the Report as a policy statement of the National Executive Committee. Apart from a new introductory section and a decision on what to do about Polaris which had been left for the NEC to resolve, the statement as adopted by the National Executive Committee was the same as that produced by the Joint Policy Committee. This statement was then put forward for consideration by the Party Conference. The NEC Statement, 'Defence and Security for Britain', was debated at the October 1984 Annual

Conference in Blackpool, and was adopted by a massive majority of four to one (5.3 million to 1.3 million on a card vote). It thus became part of the Party programme from which the Manifesto for the next General Election would be drawn.

This chapter summarises the main points of Labour's 1984 policy statement which was the basis of the policy on which Labour fought the 1987 election. However the policy was further developed by resolutions discussed at the 1985 and 1986 Conferences of the Labour Party and in particular by the NEC Statement 'Defence Conversion and Costs' adopted by the 1986 Annual Conference. This was followed by the launch in December 1986 of the 'Modern Britain in a Modern World' publicity campaign for Labour's defence and foreign policies.

'DEFENCE AND SECURITY'

'Defence and Security' represented an important watershed for the Labour Party. It made clear the Party's firm commitment to defence and collective security within NATO. At the same time it called for major changes in NATO strategy. It set out a policy for European defence and security which it subsequently further developed into common policy positions with other European socialist parties, including those in West Germany, Norway, Denmark, Belgium, the Netherlands, Spain, Portugal and Greece. In contrast to its isolationist and anti-European image in 1983 Labour now has a firmly pro-European orientation to its foreign policy. Its 1984 defence policy statement clearly played a major role in this new orientation. The whole thrust of the 1984 Report emphasised that defence policy cannot be separated from overall foreign policy. Indeed discussion of foreign policy and relations between states are fundamental to a true security policy.

'Defence and Security' was the first time that the Labour Party conference had ever set out a comprehensive defence policy statement, (as contrasted with its more usual list of resolutions expressing opposition to particular aspects of defence policy or particular weapons or strategies). The Labour Party was attempting to reconcile the strong emotional anti-nuclear sentiments it had always had and which had now grown to become a majority in terms of conference votes, with the defence and strategic arguments being put forward with increasing sophistication by academic critics of NATO's existing strategy on both sides of the Atlantic. To put it another way, 'Defence and Security' could be seen as representing an early expression of the growing convergence between the left Atlanticist views of defence intellectuals such as Labour's Foreign Affairs spokesperson and former defence minister, Denis Healey, and those of the Campaign for Nuclear Disarmament and the wider peace movement.

Labour's conference positions had originally been based on little more than a strong desire to stop cruise missiles and get rid of all nuclear weapons in Britain. But throughout the 1980s this gradually evolved into a wider policy of seeking European nuclear disarmament. Initially the evolution of a new European orientated foreign policy was confined to a small group of Parliamentarians and defence and foreign policy specialists. But by 1987 the Labour Party as a whole had (without any formal conference vote or major debate), come to terms with Britain's continuing membership of the European Community. That there was barely a murmur of opposition to the leadership's revisionism on the EEC owed a great deal to the fact that the defence policy debates had convinced many former anti-marketeers that Britain's future defence and foreign policy was inextricably bound up with the need to work with others on the European left for a new detente in Europe. Most of the democratic left now recognised that Britain needed European allies if it was to become more independent of US defence and foreign policy pressures.

With regard to security policy in general, Labour now called for policies of 'Common Security' between East and West. 'Defence and Security' pointed out that in the age of nuclear weapons true security cannot come simply from national defences or even from alliance with other countries. It is also dependent on the attitudes of the supposed adversary. Consequently countries cannot have true security alone or even in alliance. True security can only come from developing 'common security' between East and West and North and South. 'In a nuclear age no-one is secure unless we are all secure'.

MEMBERSHIP OF NATO

The 1984 Report also stated that Labour's 'long term objective is the establishment of a new security system in Europe and the mutual and concurrent phasing out of NATO and the Warsaw Pact'. But until the mutual dissolution of both blocs Labour remains firmly committed to NATO. As the Party was to state even more explicitly in the Manifesto for the 1987 General Election:

> Labour's defence policy is based squarely and firmly on Britain's membership of NATO. We are determined to make the most useful possible contribution to the alliance. We can best do that by concentrating our resources on the non-nuclear needs of our army, navy, and airforce.

The reasons for Labour's firm commitment to continuing membership of NATO are threefold. Firstly because of historical experience. As the 1987 Manifesto pointed out, 'It was a Labour Government which helped to establish the North Atlantic Alliance'. No Labour Party Conference even in the most strongly anti-nuclear years of the 1960s or the 1980s had ever got anywhere near voting for Labour to adopt a policy of British withdrawal from NATO.

Secondly as 'Defence and Security' put it 'the case for a non-nuclear defensive deterrence policy does not depend on taking a sanguine view of Soviet policy'. Indeed the 1986 NEC statement to Conference entitled 'Defence Conversion and Costs' was even more specific. It argued that: 'Central to the choices made by a Labour government on its armed forces will be an appraisal of the potential military threats facing Britain and its NATO allies'. Although the Soviet Union and its Warsaw Pact allies may have no intention of attacking Western Europe or NATO, nevertheless Labour recognised that they have a large military capability that could pose a potential military threat to Western Europe. 'Accordingly, it is only prudent that Britain and its Western European allies should maintain adequate non-nuclear defence forces capable of resisting and deterring such a potential military threat'.

Thirdly Labour recognises that Britain could have far more potential influence by using its position within NATO than it could conceivably have in the unlikely eventuality of the British people ever voting into office a government committed to leaving the Western Alliance and attempting to work from the outside. By remaining in NATO, Britain could work with other like-minded governments for policies of 'No First Use', for a battlefield nuclear weapon free zone and for a new detente with the countries of the Eastern bloc. Outside NATO it would have far less influence on either United States or European opinion.

Unlike the other political parties Labour recognises that changes within NATO are inevitable. Some two years before the October 1986 Reykjavik summit 'Defence and Security for Britain' had argued that recent disputes between European governments and the United States administration indicated that NATO was facing a deep internal crisis. The crisis was seen as an opportunity for change in Britain's relationship with the United States. Labour argued that such changes were long overdue and would be welcomed by intelligent people on both sides of the Atlantic.

Following the Reykjavik summit, the Party further developed the analysis. It pointed out that it was widely recognised on both sides of the Atlantic that the perspectives of Western Europe and the United States had changed during the previous 20 years. This divergence has produced conflicting judgements and policy disagreements. 'Just as the credibility of NATO's strategy of the 1950s (known as 'Massive Retaliation') was thrown into doubt by the development of strategic parity between the USA and USSR, so today, the strategy of the 1960s (known as 'Flexible Response') has been thrown into doubt by development of parity at lower levels ... A new strategy is needed based on a stronger and more effective conventional capability for NATO ... NATO's nuclear strategy must be changed. Reforming that strategy and re-establishing its effectiveness, requires that two conditions be met. Neither is sufficient on its own: the reliance on nuclear weapons must be brought to an end; and NATO's conventional strength must be enhanced.' (The Power to Defend Our Country, December 1986).

EUROPEAN PARTNERS

In 1984 'Defence and Security' had called for 'a new internationalist initiative' to transform relations between

NATO and the Warsaw Pact. It hoped that this could assist 'the phasing out of the cold war bloc politics into which Europe is currently frozen.' In 1984 the Party was arguing for 'a collective West European voice' in NATO which could have a strong impact on the NATO decision making process. However it was wary of any developments which might lead to the development of a 'third block' based on British and French nuclear weapons. Caution was therefore expressed about the so-called revitalisation of the Western European Union. Labour feared that the growing differences between Western Europe and the USA could lead to the development of an anti-American 'Euro-Gaullism' and the beginnings of a French-West German-British military axis based on 'independent' nuclear weapons. This would not be a step forward because it would seriously complicate international relations and make disarmament and arms control negotiations even more difficult. It would also entrench the block division in Europe.

Subsequently the Party modified this position somewhat in joint policy statements agreed by all the socialist parties in the European countries in NATO adopted at meetings in Bonn (November 1985) and Oslo (September 1986), and more significantly in the lengthy joint statement of the Labour Party and its West German sister party, the SPD, which was published in November 1986. The two parties expressed support for a 'European Pillar' in the Atlantic Alliance, but emphasised that such a pillar should be a pillar for detente, defence and disarmament and not the embryo of a new nuclear alliance or European superpower. Both parties have as a long term goal a nuclear weapon free Europe and eventual elimination of all nuclear weapons in the world. Both the British Labour Party and the West German SPD are therefore against moves towards a so-called 'European dissuasion force' or 'minimum European deterrent' or 'Euro-bomb' as advocated by some on the European right, including Dr David Owen former leader of Britain's small Social Democratic Party (not to the confused with the German SPD).

The Joint Labour-SPD Defence and Security Commission finished its work just before the launch of Labour's campaign to publicise its defence policy in December 1986.

The 'Modern Britain in a Modern World' Campaign booklet 'The Power to Defend Our Country' emphasised that:

Everything we do will involve consultation with our allies. Already discussions are under way with colleagues in Europe. In November, we agreed a joint policy with the West German Social Democratic Party. We are both committed to working together within NATO for a reduction and ultimate elimination of nuclear weapons in East and West. Both parties favour a change in NATO strategy to no first use of nuclear weapons and the need to restructure and strengthen NATO's conventional forces. The presence of the British Army of the Rhine and RAF Germany will play a vital role in this.

There are still some differences between the Labour Party and the SPD. The SPD is more cautious about taking independent or unilateral action. It is less keen than Labour on stronger conventional forces and the use of obstacles and barriers on the central front. It does not want to increase the military presence in the two German states because this might be perceived as symbolising their permanent separation. It gives great weight to its bilateral discussions with the East German ruling Socialist Unity Party and the prospects for steps of demilitarisation in central Europe. But whereas in 1980 Labour and the SPD were a very long way apart on issues like their attitude to NATO's 'Double track' decision, now they are much closer and both recognise the need to reach common positions and further develop their growing relationship in the future.

RESOURCES

The Modern Britain Campaign also emphasised the need to enhance NATO's conventional capability. Neil Kinnock had pointed out that Britain faced a choice in its defence policy between Real Defence and Nuclear Pretence. The booklet 'The Power to Defend our Country' explained: 'Britain's defences now urgently need to be restructured to meet modern demands. We need to re-shape our defence posture to make it appropriate to our role today, and commensurate with our ability to pay'. Whereas Tory plans would mean a cut of one-third in the resources available for new non-Trident equipment over the next few years, Labour in contrast would spend more on conventional forces. It would be able to do this by cancelling 'the appallingly expensive

Trident programme'. Additional savings could come from Labour's pledge to decommission the obsolescent Polaris system. The Party was also committed to 'negotiating a secure and fair settlement of the Falklands dispute which would take full account of the interests of the islanders.'

As a result of Labour's policy Britain would be able to contribute towards the enhancement of NATO's conventional forces. However, by not doing this and depriving our conventional forces Tory policy would significantly lower the nuclear threshold and increase dependence on nuclear weapons. 'The choice becomes increasingly stark as the expense of the nuclear capability persists and is met by an equally persistent - if gradual - diminishing of necessary support for the maintenance and modernisation of conventional manpower, weapons and equipment.'

The 1987 Manifesto 'Britain Will Win', pledged that a Labour Government would: 'maintain a 50 frigate and destroyer navy ... play a full part in the development of the European Fighter Aircraft ... and invest in the best up-to-date equipment for the British Army of the Rhine.'

Additional means to enhance NATO's conventional capabilities were the introduction of more rational defence procurement policies and the reforming of NATO's military strategy. 'All the evidence is that these changes, as well as helping reduce political tensions in Central Europe, would give NATO the means to contain and defeat an attack by conventional means.' (The Power to Defend Our Country.)

The spending commitments set out in the 'Modern Britain' Campaign and the 1987 Manifesto represented a shift from the wording of the 1984 document. 'Defence and Security' had already made clear that Labour believed in strong defences for Britain and NATO: 'The most important responsibility of any government is to protect and enhance the security of its citizens'. But it had not explicitly called for increases in spending on conventional forces. Instead strong emphasis had been given to the harmful economic consequences of Britain's high levels of defence spending. It had been argued that a non-nuclear defence policy could make a significant contribution to ensuring the success of Labour's economic policies.

The 1986 report to Conference developed these economic arguments. It gave detailed consideration to the military spending, weapons procurement, and arms sales aspects of the Party policy. It concluded:

> Our aim is that whilst there will be some savings in the overall levels of military spending, there will also be some resources made available to improve Britain's conventional defences. In particular, there may be a strong case for using a significant proportion of the savings on nuclear weapons expenditure to restore the short-term economies in conventional defences which the Conservatives will need to introduce to pay for Trident. As a result, in the first years of a Labour government, we recognise that some of the funds currently earmarked for nuclear and Falklands spending may have to remain within the defence budget. After a number of years, it will be realistic to expect that most of these savings could be released for use elsewhere. (Defence Conversion and Costs 1986)

However following the conference, when preparations were being made to launch the 'Modern Britain' campaign, intensive private polling and group research was carried out. The results indicated that Labour had a serious credibility problem on the defence issue. As a result in the campaign material great emphasis was put on Labour's commitment to use the savings from cancelling Trident to improve Britain's conventional defences. The qualifications and long term aspirations of the Party Conference statement were swept aside in this process. Another casualty was the strong commitment to a non-provocative 'defensive deterrence' policy. 'Defence and Security' had argued that in the nuclear age real security does not come from fighting wars but in preventing war. Security and freedom could not be defended by using nuclear weapons. Any use of nuclear weapons was likely to result in national suicide for Britain and its people. Britain's defence policy should be based on dissuasion, rather than retaliatory national suicide, with forces which were designed as unambiguously as possible for defensive purposes only. This argument for 'defensive deterrence' was down-played in the campaign. In retrospect I believe this was a mistake because it made it more difficult for Labour to argue that the Tories were grossly exaggerating the Soviet threat. It lead to an over-emphasis on the numbers of tanks, ships and planes we would build and a parallel down-playing of the political arguments for our policy. But in most other respects the Modern Britain campaign material was closely based on the statements developed over previous years.

NON-NUCLEAR MEMBERS OF NATO

In arguing for the cancellation of Trident, the de-commissioning of Polaris and the ending of Britain's 'independent' nuclear weapons, Labour pointed out that many other European countries had both the resources and the technologies to develop nuclear weapons if they wished, but had chosen not to do so. For these countries and the vast majority of countries in the world, 'independent' or national nuclear weapons are not thought necessary as a 'deterrent' to external aggression. One hundred and fifty countries in the world regard non-nuclear conventional forces, combined with economic, political, and diplomatic means as adequate deterrence against external threat. There are only five confirmed nuclear weapon states, with four or five others on the borderline.

Membership of NATO does not require member states to have nuclear weapons of their own or to allow the United States to base its nuclear weapons on their territory, or even to accede to a strategy based on the use of nuclear weapons. Already half (eight) of the sixteen member countries of the Atlantic Alliance do not allow US nuclear weapons on their territory. Denmark, Norway, Portugal, Iceland and Luxembourg have never accepted nuclear weapons. France ordered the removal of all United States forces, conventional and chemical as well as nuclear, and a NATO Headquarters, over twenty years ago. Both Spain and Canada used to allow American nuclear weapons on their territory but changed their policies in the 1970s and no longer do so. In addition, of the other NATO members, the Netherlands has unilaterally reduced the nuclear roles of its armed forces, and Greece has negotiated a Treaty involving future removal of all American nuclear weapons from its territory. Only the USA, France and Britain of the NATO countries possess so-called 'independent' nuclear weapons. So the 'typical' NATO member country is not a nuclear weapon state and it has either no nuclear weapons at all, or far fewer than it used to accept.

'Defence and Security' had called for the removal of all American nuclear bases from British territory and British territorial waters. However it had not clearly defined what it meant by a 'nuclear base'. It had also said Labour would 'regularise' the presence of the other US forces in Britain to ensure a British veto over the use of such facilities. Attempts to get motions carried by the Party conference calling for removal of all American nuclear and conventional bases and all communications facilities were opposed by the National Executive Committee and defeated by the Party Conferences in 1984, 1985 and 1986. Following the April 1986 US bombing of Libya by dual-capable F111 aircraft from British bases feelings were running very high. The National Executive Committee issued a statement four days later which said '... it shows just how vital it is for the next Labour government to re-establish British control over US bases in Britain under long-established agreements and to remove all US nuclear forces from Britain ...'. The Party Conference later that year carried a composite resolution calling for a Labour Government to negotiate an open treaty to govern the presence of the US bases and facilities in this country. The Party leader, Neil Kinnock used his speech to Conference to make clear Labour's firm commitment to a non-nuclear defence policy within NATO, but also to clarify the position that there was no plan to remove US conventional forces or their use of communications facilities such as Fylingdales.

The precise nature of the changes Labour was proposing was spelt out in his subsequent speech to the Kennedy School of Government in Boston, Massachussetts in December, and in the Modern Britain campaign material. Nuclear armed Poseidon submarines would be removed from the Holy Loch in Scotland, nuclear depth charges would be removed from their two bases in Scotland and Cornwall, nuclear bombs for the F111 would have to go from Upper Heyford and Lakenheath but the aircraft could stay in a purely conventional role, and the cruise missiles would have to go from Greenham Common and none would be permitted at the second planned base at Molesworth. The USA would still be permitted to use up to 130 bases and communications facilities for the conventional defence and reinforcement of NATO in Europe. All these changes would occur only after 'discussion' and 'consultation' with the USA and the other NATO allies, but it was made absolutely clear that the process would be completed within the lifetime of the Labour Government.

As 'The Power to Defend Our Country' argued:

And, far from incensing the Americans, at the heart of our policy is just what they so often call for: that Europe should play a greater part in its own defence. The US Congress has been pressing for some time for a strengthening of the European pillar. By bringing our view more into harmony on this question, together with the continued use by the United States of British intelligence facilities and bases in the United Kingdom and elsewhere, our links with America will be confirmed.

NATO STRATEGY AND ARMS CONTROL

'Defence and Security' had emphasised the importance of changing NATO's strategy. It saw an agreement by NATO to adopt a policy of 'No First Use' of nuclear weapons as its 'immediate goal'. This policy declaration would then be followed by changes in the manner of deployment of weapon .systems consistent with such a policy. Labour called for a new approach based on a non-provocative 'defensive deterrence' strategy.

The reasons for regarding NATO's existing strategy as unworkable have already been given. As the Party put it in 'The Power to Defend Our Country':

> In the sure knowledge of what it would do to ourselves, and our country for generations, is it reasonable to believe any longer that either we, or the Americans, would launch nuclear weapons to halt a Soviet invasion of Europe? That crucial question has compelled people of the status and experience of Robert McNamara, former American Secretary of Defence, to conclude that he knows of no plan which gives reasonable assurance that nuclear weapons can be used beneficially in NATO's defence. Admiral of the Fleet Lord Mountbatten took the same view.

Once a No First Use strategy had been agreed, Labour would then press for NATO to open negotiations with the Warsaw Pact to establish a continent-wide European nuclear weapon free zone. This could build on the ideas first proposed in the Rapacki Plan put forward by the Polish Foreign Minister in the 1950s, on the more recent efforts by the governments of Norway, Sweden, Finland and Denmark to establish a Nordic nuclear weapon free zone and on the so far less well developed ideas of a similar nature for the Balkans and the Iberian peninsula. Above all it could encompass the ideas put forward by the Palme Commission in 1982 and subsequently embodied in the draft treaties for a chemical weapon free zone and a battlefield nuclear weapon free corridor in both German states and Czechoslovakia, as agreed in 1985 and 1986 by the West German SPD and the ruling party in East Germany, the SED.

In the words of 'Defence and Security',

> A nuclear weapons-free Europe could make a major contribution to peace and security in the world. Our aim is the creation of different forms of international organisation and a new internationalist politics. In Europe, this means working for the establishment of a European nuclear-weapon free zone and a new European-wide security system, leading to the ultimate replacement of the present division of Europe into NATO and the Warsaw Pact by the dissolution of the two blocks.

Labour argues that reliance on an outdated strategy has provided Britain and NATO as a whole with an excuse for failing to take the steps needed to enhance conventional strength.

> It is vital that Britain makes a concrete first step towards the implementation of a non-nuclear defence strategy. Without it, the need for change is likely to remain at the level of academic speculation. That is why it is our intention to cancel Trident, de-commission Polaris and remove all American nuclear weapons in this country. Only by doing this will we be believed when we argue for less reliance on nuclear weapons in the NATO alliance. (The Power to Defend Our Country)

The long term policy of the Labour Party is for the removal of all nuclear weapons in the world. This goal is consistent with the statements of both Ronald Reagan and Mikhail Gorbachev and the goals set out at their historic October 1986 meeting in Reykjavik where they discussed removal of all cruise missiles from Europe, a 50% cut in strategic warheads and a global ban on all ballistic nuclear missiles in ten years. General Secretary Gorbachev says he wants to eliminate all nuclear weapons within the remaining years of this century. President Reagan has said nuclear weapons are evil and must never be used. He says he wants to make them impotent and obsolete. The declaratory statements of these two world leaders contrast sharply with the stated policy of Mrs Thatcher that she wants to continue to rely on nuclear deterrence for the indefinite future. She told the Soviet people in March 1987 that she was not prepared to accept the de-nuclearisation of Europe.

A similar nationalistic policy is to be found across the Channel in France, where it is even supported by the parties of the left. The present Governments in Britain and France are a serious impediment to achieving the aspiration of the overwhelming majority of world opinion of establishing a world free from the threat of nuclear apocalypse.

Labour sees independent steps by Britain as helping to achieve international arms control and disarmament. However, as the 1984 Report made very clear: 'We are realists. The process of disarmament will not occur overnight: it will be brought about by a process of independent steps by individual countries and by international agreements following patient negotiations. We will work to build trust and detente and make strenuous efforts to improve the international climate and, step by step, contribute to greater security for Britain and the world'. Just as the arms race is a spiral of independent actions and reactions, so the process of disarmament will be fostered by independent steps of de-escalation. An historic example of such a step of de-escalation was President Kennedy's 1963 announcement of a unilateral US halt to testing nuclear weapons in the atmosphere. This independent/unilateral step was the key to a subsequent improvement in US-Soviet relations and the 1963 Partial Nuclear Test Ban Treaty. A positive Western response to the unilateral Soviet moratorium on nuclear tests in 1985-7 could have led to an early agreement on a comprehensive nuclear test ban treaty. Instead the USA, Britain and France all carried on testing and an historic opportunity was lost.

However independent steps can only make a limited contribution. Neither the USA nor the USSR will give up their nuclear weapons whilst the other possesses nuclear weapons. But it would be in their interests and the interests of the peoples of Europe and the world if the two superpowers were to scale down sharply the level of their nuclear arsenals and eventually agree to their elimination.

When Labour adopted its 1984 statement prospects for any arms control agreement between the superpowers were very slight. But the Reykjavik meeting in late 1986 changed that. This led to a movement in the position of the Labour leadership concerning the unilateral removal of cruise missiles from Britain. In early 1987 just before his visit to the USA to meet President Reagan, Neil Kinnock made clear that as long as there were good prospects for a speedy agreement to remove all intermediate nuclear missiles from Europe, Labour would do nothing in or out of government which could undermine the chances of such a negotiated agreement. The attitude of the Labour Party to the arms control and disarmament negotiations was spelt out as follows in the 1987 General Election Manifesto:

> We have always recognised that a properly negotiated and monitored international agreement to remove nuclear weapons from European soil would provide the most effective guarantee against the horrors of nuclear war. It would be the most significant step towards an eventual world-wide renunciation of, and ban upon, nuclear weapons. That is why we were the first to propose to the super-powers the zero option in respect of intermediate nuclear weapons. Labour therefore strongly supports the talks between the United States and Soviet governments aimed at reducing nuclear armaments. Success in these efforts to negotiate the removal of all' intermediate nuclear missiles in Europe would be warmly welcomed. It would mean the removal of America's cruise missiles here in Britain and in the rest of Europe as well as Pershing IIs in Germany and the Soviet SS20's and other shorter range missiles. We naturally, therefore, want to assist that process in every way possible. If, however, it should fail, we shall, after consultation, inform the Americans that we wish them to remove their Cruise missiles and other nuclear missiles from Britain. We would then become the ninth - of the sixteen NATO members - which do not have US nuclear weapons on their territory. This change would of course not affect the other US, British and joint defence and early warning systems in the United Kingdom.

Labour wants Britain to use its collective roles in NATO as leverage to help achieve a defensive conventional posture for NATO in Europe, building support amongst sympathetic NATO partners and within the NATO decision making structure. This would be assisted by making the British Ambassador to NATO a direct political appointment.

> We are working for a defensive conventional posture for NATO. Such a posture need not differ substantially from NATO's present conventional posture. It would be desirable to remove some obviously 'offensive' elements and to strengthen the 'defensive' emphasis. It would also be beneficial to phase out the very expensive oversophisticated weapons systems. There may also be advantages in greater in-depth defence in Germany. (Defence and Security)

Labour recognises that strengthening NATO's conventional defences and relieving the USA of the unrealistic obligation to commit nuclear suicide in response to a Soviet conventional attack on Western Europe is fully supported by many Americans. Adoption of No First Use would be very popular on both sides of the Atlantic. It would also make military sense.

Labour has also called for collective European pressure for detente and disarmament and for European participation in the arms control negotiations.

MILITARY REFORMS

'Defence and Security' stressed the importance of 'fundamental military reform' in NATO. It argued that the most important and necessary reform of all is the removal of nuclear weapons from the Central Front. This will in itself release resources to enhance NATO's conventional defences. It was seen as a pre-condition for moving to an effective, non-suicidal defence for NATO.

These ideas were considered in greater detail in the 1986 statement 'Defence Conversion and Costs', and were incorporated in the 'Modern Britain' Campaign booklet, 'The Power to Defend Our Country':

> For too long, our reliance on nuclear weapons has led NATO to neglect vital consideration of military strategy. A strategy which would depend on the firing of nuclear weapons once the front line is breached, is not tenable. As a first step - and one that already has wide support - all nuclear and chemical weapons should be withdrawn from a corridor 150 kilometres deep on both sides of the dividing line ... Concurrently we must lead the move in NATO for greater defence in depth,

enabling our forces to capitalise properly on the intrinsic tactical advantage that defensive forces hold over offensive ones.

Labour called for 'better use of NATO's existing reserves of trained manpower', deployment of 'man-made barriers and obstacles', and 'use of new technologies to improve defensive weapons'. '(This) is better than spending money on weapons which may not work for deep strike against targets which may not be there. Modern defensive weaponry and Precision Guided Munitions give greater advantages to the defence'.

Air force and naval reforms would also be needed to accompany the change on the Central Front. Associated with this would be new policies for defence procurement. Whilst expressing a strong commitment to maintaining Britain's defence industrial base, Labour also called for 'stricter control over arms manufacturers' and more 'open government' through greater parliamentary scrutiny of procurement. This would 'help to reduce costs and allow purchase of a larger number of less expensive weapons ... The emphasis in procurement must move back towards simple, cheaper and more reliable weaponry'.

The military reforms called for by Labour are both affordable and relevant. They would also send out the right kind of political signals. Following the important agreements on Confidence-building measures at Stockholm in September 1986, there is now an opening for an agreement to reduce and restructure the conventional forces of both NATO and the Warsaw Pact. The Soviet Union under Mikhail Gorbachev seems to have become receptive to such ideas. The tragedy is that so far internal divisions in NATO and old-fashioned attitudes have led the West to drag its feet. Labour is opposed to the new 'Deep Strike' concepts like the US Army's 'AirLand Battle' doctrine which, as Andrew Kelly points out elsewhere in this book, commit the West to dangerous and destabilising strategies which do little to enhance conventional deterrence. As 'Defence and Security' argued in 1984:

From the Soviet viewpoint, the ability of NATO to seize terrain well into Eastern European territory would be perceived as part of a political and military offensive strategy for NATO ... Defence policy should not send out the wrong political signals to a potential enemy. A policy of defensive deterrence is not compatible with an offensive military posture such as proposed in the new 'deep strike' strategies.

WINNING SUPPORT

It is of course one thing to develop a comprehensive and costed policy, however coherent and logical, and quite another to be able to successfully sell it to the public. Between 1979 and 1983 Labour's internal civil war had left no time or energy for anything else. After 1983 the whole movement was aware that it could not repeat such introspective sectarianism. It was also widely felt particularly by peace movement activists in the Labour Party that the newly agreed defence and particularly the disarmament policies should be put across in a coherent campaign to be launched well before the next General Election. As we have seen the basis of the new policy was already established in 1984, although further embellishment occurred over the next two years.

The Party Conference had called for such a public campaign as early as 1985 but nothing was done until after the 1986 Conference had repeated the call, and after the Chernobyl disaster and the US bombing of Libya from British bases had heightened public concern about these issues, temporarily resulting in a big surge in opposition to all things nuclear as registered in opinion polls that summer.

However it was not entirely surprising that the Labour Party should have delayed launching any public high-profile campaign until the end of 1986. Some senior officials at Walworth Road were worried that doing anything at all to campaign on defence policy might open up a repetition of the damaging splits experienced in 1983. In addition the Labour Party does have a serious resource allocation problem and there was a great deal of scepticism as to how effective yet another 'national campaign' would be. So there was initially strong resistance to the idea. However, once the decision had been made to go ahead, considerable human and financial resources were put into the campaign and there was an intensive period of activity involving many people from all departments at Walworth Road and outside volunteer and contract staff, in what was widely recognised to be a sophisticated, professional and quite effective campaign.

The aims of the 'Modern Britain in a Modern World' Campaign were two-fold. Firstly to set out Labour's policies in the overall context of the foreign policy of the Party, and secondly to counter the public misconceptions that Labour would leave Britain defenceless. It was recognised that this was a high-risk strategy, but it was felt, rightly in my view, that it was better to attempt to do this early and in doing so prepare the party and its leading figures well in advance of a general election rather than try to ignore the issue and risk a repeat of the discordant debacle of 1983. In those terms the campaign must be judged a partial success. It did shift public opinion to recognising that Labour believed in strong conventional forces. It did contribute to a much greater cohesion and coherence in the statements of leading figures from all wings of the Party and it laid the basis for overwhelming unity on the defence policy put forward in the election Manifesto 'Britain Will Win' which was published at the start of the General Election Campaign in May 1987.

What all these developments could not do was to ensure Labour's victory on June 11th 1987. Despite fighting what was widely recognised to be the best campaign and clearly re-establishing its credibility as the only alternative government, the Labour Party under Neil Kinnock was only able to make a partial dent in the huge Tory majority. The reasons for this were many and complex. The election was mainly fought - and rightly so - on social and economic policies. It was lost on economic and social policies. Labour undoubtedly suffered from its association with 'extremism' in local government and also lost support on economic and taxation policies.

However defence policy was an important issue. In contrast to 1983 Labour gained rather than lost support overall during the campaign. However, opinion polling indicates that up to a quarter of voters in Labour's target seats gave our policy on nuclear weapons as the main reason why they were deterred from supporting Labour. This was a far higher proportion than on any other single issue. It reached a peak in the middle of the campaign when the saliency of the issue had been raised by Neil Kinnock's statement during his interview by David Frost that occupation of Britain was untenable. These remarks were distorted and blown up into headlines in the Tory press about 'Fighting in the streets' and 'Kinnock advocates guerrilla warfare'. This was a total misrepresentation of Labour's policy of stronger conventional forces on the Central Front in Germany which could resist and repel any invasion threat well before it got anywhere near this country. But it was effective nevertheless.

There is no evidence that Labour actually lost support overall on the defence issue during the campaign, in marked contrast to 1983. Perhaps that was because some potential support had already been lost when the Party launched its Modern Britain Campaign and following Neil Kinnock's two highly publicised visits to the USA in December 1986 and March 1987. Some pollsters have claimed that up to three per cent more voters might have been won by Labour if it had put forward a different defence policy in the election Manifesto. They fail to explain what that policy should have been or more pertinently how the Party could have credibly dropped one of its most important policies without causing a very damaging internal split on a par with what happened in 1983 which would almost certainly have led to the loss of even more support.

Similar objections could also be made to those who propose a referendum on the issue. This could easily be portrayed as a sign of weakness, indecisiveness and internal division. There would also be a serious problem deciding what issues to put in the referendum - Polaris? Trident? US nuclear weapons? NATO? Conventional spending? The size of the surface fleet? And who would reconcile contradictory answers if for example the people voted simultaneously to keep British nuclear weapons, cancel Trident but have a nuclear successor to Polaris, spend no more on defence than current levels but strengthen conventional forces. The referendum would rightly be seen as a cop out. A proposal for such a referendum was defeated resoundingly by both the Trades Union Congress and the Labour Party Conferences in 1987.

In fact despite attacks on its policies orchestrated by its opponents and given extensive coverage in an overwhelmingly hostile national press, Labour remained firmly united behind its policies and did not fall apart on the defence issue as it had done with such painful damage to its credibility in 1983.

The Conservative and SDP/Liberal Alliance campaigns concentrated their fire on Labour's commitment to decommission the ageing Polaris system. Both parties pandered to crude nationalistic emotions rather than engaging in rational discussion about how best to defend Britain and Europe. It has to be admitted that they had some success. The sad fact is that on defence issues most people are not willing to listen to rational or logical arguments. Research indicates that most people would rather not think or talk about these issues at all. When forced to do so they frequently fall back on crude stereotypes and emotional responses. Einstein said that nuclear weapons had changed everything except the way men (sic) think. It appears that in Britain at least little has changed in the last forty years in this respect. As long as the British people see nuclear weapons as a kind of national status symbol then it will be extremely difficult to introduce a coherent and rational defence policy to this country.

THE NEXT ELECTION

It will be another four or five years before Neil Kinnock's revitalised Labour Party is able to complete the job of winning power. Those four or five years will inevitably see further changes in the international environment. A double-zero option agreement on intermediate and shorter range nuclear missiles could be followed by negotiations to reduce or remove battlefield nuclear weapons from central Europe along the lines proposed by the Palme Commission. A 50% cut in the strategic arsenals of the two superpowers could be agreed alongside restrictions on the development phase of the Strategic Defence Initiative. The Gorbachev perestroika could lead to fundamental changes in Eastern Europe with big implications for the two German states and for the relationship between NATO and the Warsaw Pact. The USA could well cut its troop strength in Europe and the Soviet armed forces could be reduced and restructured, both of these being carried out for internal economic reasons which have very little to do with conventional balance of power arguments. All these changes would fit in well with an optimistic scenario which could make Labour's existing policies on defence and disarmament even more relevant and necessary than they were in 1987.

On the other hand by 1991 if the Tories carry on with Trident they will have spent or committed the bulk of its £10 billion cost (at 1986 prices). They will have slashed the Royal Navy and cut new equipment for the other two services to pay for Trident. Labour's arguments in the 1987 campaign will be vindicated. But that will be of little consolation to the workers in Britain's conventional defence industries. In 1991 we will not be able to make many extra resources available for our army, navy and airforce by cancelling Trident. The savings will already have been wasted by Tory nuclearphilia. Of course President Reagan could solve the problem for us by pursuing his Reykjavik proposal to ban all ballistic missiles, including Trident, by 1996, but in those circumstances the present British Government would probably choose to spend even more on a French nuclear missile rather than join in the process towards the elimination of nuclear weapons in Europe and the world.

Whatever happens in the next five years it seems inevitable that changing circumstances will require some modifications and further development of Labour's non-nuclear defence policy. Indeed the 1987 Party Conference has already voted for a review of the timetable and negotiating strategy for implementing Labour's non-nuclear defence policy within NATO. But events could also make it much easier to sell that policy to the British electorate - particularly if it is seen more clearly to be going with the grain of world and European opinion than it was in 1987.

REFERENCES

The New Hope for Britain. The Labour Party Election Manifesto, 1983

Defence and Security for Britain. National Executive Committee Statement to Annual Conference, The Labour Party, 1984

Defence Conversion and Costs, National Executive Committee Statement to Annual Conference, The Labour Party, 1986

The Power to Defend Our Country. Pamphlet published as part of the Modern Britain in a Modern World Campaign, The Labour Party, 1986

Britain Will Win, The Labour Party Election Manifesto, 1987

Chapter Five

A NON-NUCLEAR, NON-NATO BRITAIN: IS THERE AN ELECTORAL PATHWAY?

Patrick Dunleavy

How likely is it that British voters in the coming decade will support radical moves to denuclearise the United Kingdom, to regain complete control of British armed forces for their own elected government, and to shift decisively towards a de-aligned position in the military rivalry between the USA and the Soviet Union? For most experts on defence policy, and for the vast majority of pundits who analyse British public opinion, the answers to these questions will seem transparently obvious. Despite the progress in 1986-7 towards the effective denuclearisation of Europe with the likely removal of US and Soviet short and intermediate range nuclear missiles, the evidence of the 1983 and 1987 elections seems to confirm the British electorate's continuing determination to retain a British nuclear deterrent. The conventional wisdom holds that British voters are now very unlikely ever to give majority endorsement to a non-nuclear defence stance.

Obviously official Labour party sources disagree, although many Parliamentary leaders of the party remain convinced that getting rid of nuclear weapons from British territory is hardly a vote-getting issue for the party to promote. A slightly broader spectrum of media and 'expert' opinion is now beginning to support Labour's case against a nuclear deterrent in terms of setting priorities for Britain's limited defence resources, while insisting that a useful function is served by retaining US nuclear bases on British soil. By contrast with this increasingly lively debate on official Labour policy, (almost) everyone agrees that any party which envisages coming out of NATO would be massacred at the polls. A dissenting view is seriously put forward only by the Labour 'hard' left, for whom US policy appears just as menacing as that of the Soviet Union. Together with a few committed pacifists they solemnly proclaim the willingness of the British electorate to quickly adopt completely different majority attitudes if only the Labour leadership had the political will to offer a resolute and determined moral lead against the whole fabric of both the NATO alliance and the nuclear arms race.

This chapter tries to show why both the polarised positions of the pro-nuclear/pro-NATO conventional wisdom and of the anti-nuclear/anti-NATO hard left are inadequate. Since Mike Gapes sets out official Labour policy at length in Chapter 4, and discusses the feasibility of getting it implemented, I largely leave this partial dissent from the conventional wisdom out of the analysis which follows. In the first section I argue against the conventional wisdom and the anti-NATO left that sustained denuclearisation and uncoupling of British policy from nuclear alliances can only be envisaged as a 'rolling programme'. It will need to be created stage by stage over a lengthy period (of perhaps two decades), building at each stage on existing popular support for further measures of piecemeal denuclearisation. In the second section I explore the evidence about British voters' complex attitudes towards alternative defence policies, showing what the potential for progress to denuclearisation may be under current (mid 1987) political conditions. Finally in the third section I examine a number of scenarios for implementing a rolling programme of denuclearisation, with particular reference to the political conditions succeeding the next general election - or perhaps the next two elections if, as seems quite likely, the political parties prove unable to adapt quickly to minority government or coalition situations.

THREE VIEWS OF DENUCLEARISATION

The conventional view of British public attitudes towards nuclear weapons and alliances is shared by the mass media, most Parliamentarians (including a substantial minority of Labour MPs), and of course the defence establishment itself. This position argues that public attitudes towards nuclear weapons have been extraordinarily stable throughout the post-war period, with large majority support for an independent British nuclear deterrent, apparently very little influenced by the campaigns of CND and the peace movement either in the 1960s or the 1980s. When British voters were offered clear opportunities to choose between parties supporting or opposing the nuclear deterrent at the 1983 and 1987 elections, they overwhelmingly rejected change, with apparently damaging implications for the Labour vote. Moreover, large majorities in opinion polls have consistently supported British membership of NATO, including the use of nuclear weapons in retaliation for a nuclear attack on Britain. Public attitudes towards the detailed conduct of American foreign policy are much more ambiguous, however, with public suspicion of Reagan's Presidency particularly marked. And the siting of US cruise missiles at bases in mainland Britain has always provoked as much public dissent as support.

The committed anti-NATO view discounts the evidence of existing majority support for maintaining the nuclear deterrent by pointing out the implausibility of supposing that public opinion could have adopted any other configuration for most of the post-war period. With the Labour party and the trade union movement committed for all but a brief period in 1961 to nuclear deterrence, and with even the radical-sounding Labour manifesto commitment of 1964 promptly sold out by the party leadership when they gained power, how could voters' views have been otherwise? Similarly the two 1980s election results in this view reflect the party's relatively recent adoption of a non-nuclear posture. In 1983 there were fatal divisions inside the Labour leadership about the policy, which resurfaced during the election campaign itself. In 1987 there was relatively little sign that Labour was badly damaged by the issue during the campaign, most of which focused on economic and welfare state issues. With a more favourable international climate in East-West relations in prospect, a longer time period to sell a principled nuclear disarmament to voters, and with the eradication of half-hearted unilateralists from the party leadership, the hard left argue that majority electoral support for a non-nuclear posture can be successfully built up by a strong campaigning party even while it is in opposition. The main difficulty will lie in trying to persuade voters of the moral and practical case for denuclearisation while attempting to remain also within NATO - which is fundamentally an anti-Soviet nuclear alliance. On this view current Labour policy (as set out by Mike Gapes in Chapter 4) contains electorally dangerous contradictions, making it acutely vulnerable to destabilising interventions by the US administration and conservative forces in both the UK and other European NATO countries. Even if short term electoral costs might be incurred, the longer term prospects for nuclear disarmament are better served by moving immediately to a strong campaigning stance pledged to pull the UK out of NATO altogether.

In my view there are points of plausibility in both the conventional view and the anti-NATO approach. The conventional account correctly summarises the immense inertial weight of existing public attitudes towards nuclear disarmament. It is also right to stress that even if it can ever be inaugurated denuclearisation will be a multi-stage process, likely to span more than one Parliament. Hence it is potentially reversible by an incoming Conservative government, as well as being open to blockage by NATO allies and foot-dragging by the British defence establishment. But the hard left are also right to stress that voters cannot adopt non-nuclear attitudes on their own, and that campaigning by a major political party carries vastly more weight than could CND activities in their period of combatting a united front by all the major political parties. Equally there is some considerable evidence of misgivings and tensions underlying majority voter support for a British deterrent and the NATO alliance.

My third view of the prospects for denuclearisation combines these plausible elements into a more complex account in which a non-nuclear commitment is seen as a viable but longer term project. It cannot be a snap-shot policy, capable of being accomplished by achieving a single Labour parliamentary majority. Instead it will of necessity have the characteristics of a rolling programme, which must be tackled stage by stage, maintaining a delicate balance between respect for voters' existing attitudes and adopting a campaigning stance designed to change those attitudes.

The rolling programme concept also acknowledges a point accorded primary importance in recent work on the theory of party competition, namely that the party of government can exercise a far more decisive influence upon the structure of public opinion than can opposition parties (Dunleavy and Ward, 1981; Dunleavy and Husbands, 1985, pp.46-52). All political parties have a limited capacity for 'opinion leadership', chiefly manifested by the tendency for voters who become committed to supporting a party to adjust their views of individual issues so as to make them fit

109

in more closely with the party's programme. But the incumbent party of government is in a position to actually shape the objective situation of voters far more directly and dramatically than can opposition parties. For example, the conduct of economic policies and the patriotic rallying effect of involvement in the Falklands War have both been credited with the dramatic rallying of support for the Conservative government in the spring and summer of 1982.

Securing access to government power is particularly crucial in setting a rolling programme in motion, allowing it to accumulate the momentum which can ensure that it becomes self-sustaining. An appropriate analogy here is the Conservative's privatisation programme, which scarcely featured in their 1979 manifesto, but which has step by step gathered momentum to become the centrepiece of Thatcher's second and third terms. The hallmark of a rolling programme of this kind is that the party pursuing it must manage a controlled release of information about its stance, progressively pushing back the frontiers of public acceptability but without risking alienating or alarming large numbers of voters by adopting threatening positions which cannot be immediately implemented. A rolling programme requires party leaders to practice a form of strategic decision-making with some implications which run counter to much common sense reasoning. For example, the pace of policy change will tend to be relatively circumspect when the party is in opposition, but to speed up in government when the incumbent party is able to put the full weight of the state apparatus behind efforts to shift public perceptions.

In assessing the plausibility of sustaining a rolling programme of denuclearisation, we must move away from a simple calculation of the degree to which current public opinion supports particular policy positions and instead focus on two critical issues. First, will sufficient voters ever support the defence policies of a party committed to a non-nuclear position to allow the rolling programme to get started? In the context of current British politics this question reduces to the electoral chances of a majority Labour government, with perhaps an outside chance of a few unilateralist Alliance or Nationalist MPs lending their support should a minority Labour government seek to begin serious disarmament moves in a hung Parliament. Second, assuming that a rolling programme of denuclearisation could be initiated (for example, by scrapping all nuclear weapons barring the main Trident/Polaris system in operation as the principal UK deterrent, and by expelling US nuclear bases) what evidence is there that public opinion on defence issues could be persuaded to accept further movement towards full withdrawal from the nuclear arms race and the alliances which sustain it?

PUBLIC ATTITUDES TOWARDS DENUCLEARISATION

Assessing public attitudes towards a complex of policy questions such as these is by no means as straightforward as the conventional view would have us believe for four reasons. First, in defence policy as much as in other issue areas public responses to opinion poll questions vary quite considerably depending upon the precise question wording employed. However, most polling organisations are commissioned to undertake research by newspapers or interest groups which characteristically focus upon at most one or two questions. Second, those polling organisations which maintain an over-time series of polls, with constant question wording employed over several years to gauge changes in public opinion, typically focus on a single question as the basis for their series. Third, the sampling of the electorate's views on specific issues, even those as important as nuclear weapons, is rather episodic. At periods (such as elections) when the issue is in the news poll evidence is plentiful. But outside these periods, when non-nuclear defence is not on the agenda of the incumbent government, then we may only be able to guess at constancy in public attitudes. Fourth, it is often very difficult to determine the meaning and significance which should be attached to particular configurations of public attitudes because of the existence of strong opinion leadership influences, where voters adjust their attitudes on an issue to bring them into line with those of a party they have chosen to support for other reasons.

This effect implies that the issue attitudes on nuclear weapons will be 'contaminated' by quite general voter evaluations of the political parties, especially during a general election campaign when voters' commitments to particular parties firm up greatly and when opinion leadership effects are consequently at their strongest. On the other hand opinion polls carried out in the mid-terms between elections are equally difficult to assess because

Table 5.1: The Gallup and MORI time series data on attitudes towards nuclear disarmament

GALLUP

Percentage giving a:	1980 Sep	'81 Nov	'82 Nov	'83 Feb	Date of Poll May	Jun	Nov	1986 Jul	Aug*	1987 Jan
Pro-nuclear response	67	58	61	65	66	73	67	57	46	55
Anti-nuclear response	21	33	29	28	27	20	23	33	44	35
Don't know	11	9	10	6	7	7	10	9	10	11
Pro-nuclear majority	46	25	32	37	39	53	44	24	2	20

MORI

Percentage giving a:	1981 Oct	1983 Jan	Date of poll Mar	May	Oct	1986 Nov
Pro-nuclear response	69	72	62	72	73	63
Anti-nuclear response	23	23	32	19	25	31
Don't know	8	5	6	9	2	6
Pro-nuclear majority	46	49	30	53	48	32

Note: For question wording see text
* = slightly changed question wording

Sources: Gallup Political Index, no. 270, table 13; no. 273, Table 7; no. 274, Table 20; no. 279, Table 12; no. 312, Table 12; no. 313, Table 16; July 1987, Table 12; MORI newsletter, British Public Opinion, November/December 1986, volume VII, no. 10, p.5.

they give voters' responses only to rather 'academic' questions. Voters may well be more willing to embrace policy innovations in an opinion poll (or a bye-election) which has no chance of directly affecting government policy than in a general election where their vote collectively determines the composition of the new government.

The best long term evidence available about British public attitudes to denuclearisation is given by responses to a question sporadically included in Gallup's political questions poll, which asks: 'It has been suggested that Britain should give up relying on nuclear weapons for defence whatever other countries decide. Do you think this is a good idea or a bad idea?' This question is biased in two ways towards a 'bad idea' response. The phrase 'give up relying on nuclear weapons' presents denuclearisation in a negative way, without mentioning any substitute for nuclear weapons spending. And the phrase 'whatever other countries decide' is a strong one. Table 5.1 shows how the electorate has responded.

It is clear that there has always been a pro-nuclear majority on this question, with the exception of a single poll in the summer of 1986. Compared with the 1980 figures, those for 1981 and 1982 showed a variable but lower pro-nuclear majority, unsurprisingly given the deteriorating East-West climate in this period and the Labour party's shift towards a unilateralist disarmament posture at its October 1981 Conference. From the autumn of 1982 until May 1983 there was a gradual reversal of this trend, mainly achieved by people shifting out of the 'don't know' category into a pro-nuclear response, possibly reflecting also a slight improvement in US-Soviet relations. During the June 1983 election campaign, however, when Labour under Michael Foot handled the nuclear issue exceptionally badly, the pro-nuclear majority grew dramatically and the support for a unilateralist position apparently slumped badly (see Dunleavy and Husbands, 1985, pp.89-91, 16-64). Although the East-West climate began to improve quite appreciably throughout 1983 (and despite the deployment of Cruise missiles in Britain in the autumn) the high levels of pro-nuclear responses recorded in June quickly ebbed away to recreate a picture much more in line with earlier responses.

The figures for 1986 in Table 5.1 apparently show a major turnround in public attitudes, with the pro-nuclear majority on this question virtually disappearing by August. The trigger for this change can be relatively easily pinpointed. In April 1986 the Chernobyl nuclear power plant in the Soviet Union exploded, releasing a cloud of radioactive contamination which spread across much of Western Europe including Britain in the succeeding three weeks. An NOP poll conducted within a month of this incident recorded a large increase in the numbers of people giving a 'unilateralist' response to a differently worded question. Gallup's two polls for July and August 1986 separated by three politically uneventful weeks show a big increase in the numbers giving an anti-nuclear response. The August poll showing the virtual disappearance of a pro-nuclear majority is especially different from previous results, but it uses a slightly varied question (suggested by CND which commissioned this particular poll). The revised form of wording was: 'Do you agree or disagree that Britain should get rid of its nuclear weapons whatever other countries do?' By January 1987 the same wording was again showing a pro-nuclear majority, although with a higher anti-nuclear response (35 per cent) and only just over a half of respondents firmly attached to the nuclear deterrent. These results are consistent with some other recent commentaries, such as the British Social Attitudes Survey, where Paul Whiteley concluded: 'Our data suggest that an anti-nuclear stance is becoming more prevalent, though slowly' (Whiteley, 1985, p.111).

However, given the limitations of any single poll question, it is worthwhile looking also at a question used sporadically by MORI since 1981, which runs:

> I am going to read out to you a number of policies that some people would like the next government to adopt. For each would you tell me whether you support or oppose each policy? ... Get rid of all nuclear weapons in Britain even if other countries keep theirs.

Again this is a pretty clearly biased form of wording, for it presents denuclearisation as simply 'getting rid of' something without mentioning compensating· positive changes in defence policy. And instead of the 'whatever other countries decide' formulation used by Gallup, there is the phrase 'even if other countries keep theirs' - which rather strongly .suggests a threat involved in denuclearisation. Asking about 'all nuclear weapons' also composites together British and American weapons. Predictably enough given this slanting the MORI question has always shown a pro-nuclear majority in 1981, 1983 and 1986. The evidence of an opinion leadership effect at the time of the 1983 election strengthening the pro-nuclear consensus is apparent, although the March 1983 MORI result seems to be a 'blip' result. Again there are no data for 1984 or 1985, but there is evidence of a growth of anti-nuclear sentiment in the October 1986 figures. The profile of responses in 1986 shows large majorities of Conservative and Alliance supporters giving pro-nuclear responses, but a majority of Labour supporters favouring non-nuclear policies.

Turning to the 1987 general election itself, defence was the second most frequently cited issue in Gallup's question about which policy questions affected people's vote. The importance of defence was little changed from its 1983 level at 35 per cent, while the top issue, unemployment, rated at 49 instead of 72 per cent (Crewe, 1987). The overwhelming majority of people citing defence as important preferred the Conservative's policies. Amongst voters as a whole the Conservatives were cited by more than twice as many people as Labour as the party with the best defence policies (Gallup Political Index, July 1987), although their lead on the issue did not grow markedly during the campaign, unlike 1983. People who were not voting Labour were asked by Gallup to indicate their reasons, one of which was tapped by the statement: 'Labour's defence policy is dangerous'. The proportion of non-Labour voters choosing this view rose from 21 per cent at the start of the campaign to 52 per cent by the final days. Of course, a somewhat similar pattern of change took place on other responses, as non-Labour voters became more practised at justifying their stance to pollsters. But on average the other response items on Gallup's list showed only a doubling of mentions, whereas the mentions of dangerous defence policies multiplied two and a half times.

One of the problems with all the data considered so far is that single poll questions may not adequately catch the complexity of public attitudes. To find evidence based on multiple poll questions we need to turn back to a survey carried out by the LSE Election Studies Unit in the three weeks immediately after the June 1983 election, the low point of support for non-nuclear policies during the 1980s. The poll used a nationally representative quota sample of 1023 respondents, and included six defence questions designed to be slanted in different directions and to try and surface ambiguities in public attitudes towards nuclear weapons.

Two questions produced decisive majorities, agreeing that Britain should negotiate to reduce nuclear weapons holdings with the Soviet Union, and disagreeing that Britain

Table 5.2: Responses to Six Attitude Questions on Nuclear Defence, LSE Election Study 1983

	Overall agree	Strongly agree	Tend to agree	Tend to disagree	Strongly disagree
1. Britain should seek to negotiate with the Russians in order to reduce both sides' holdings of nuclear weapons	86	47	39	9	5
2. Given the state of the arms race, it is necessary for Britain to introduce new types of nuclear weapons	57	19	38	20	22
3. Britain should keep the nuclear weapons it has now, but should not introduce any new types of nuclear weapons	51	19	32	33	16
4. Britain should continue to allow its territory to be used by the United States as a base from which American nuclear weapons could be launched	47	16	31	21	32
5. Britain should base its defence on a strong conventional army, navy and air force, without any nuclear weapons	42	19	23	39	19
6. Britain should get rid of its own nuclear weapons, irrespective of what other countries do	17	8	8	24	59

should get rid of its own nuclear weapons whatever other countries do. The remaining four questions showed a much more evenly balanced degree of agreement or disagreement. Some immediate effects of question wording can be detected. The level of agreement with a non-nuclear policy is nearly three times as great when it is linked with the need for strong conventional armed forces than when it is associated with Labour's perceived 1983 policy of unilateralism come what may.

In trying to assess the prospects for changes in this 1983 pattern of attitudes, Chris Husbands has suggested that it is important to explore how voters' responses to questions about nuclear defence hang together (Dunleavy and Husbands, 1985, pp.175-80). The more consistent voters' attitudes are, the less likely they are to change their minds - whereas if people hold fairly confused views initially they may be more open to opinion leadership influences. The LSE election study found that voters held more consistent views about nuclear defence than about some other key issues in the 1983 campaign, such as the forms of provision of welfare services. Husbands used quite a strong test for consistency, arguing that people's responses to the second, third and sixth questions in Table 5.1 above should logically hang together. Table 5.3 shows that the biggest bloc of consistent voters in 1983 were those who preferred Britain to introduce new nuclear weapons, while simultaneously rejecting policies of adhering to the status quo or of pursuing nuclear disarmament.

By contrast less than one in ten voters gave consistently unilateralist opinions, disagreeing with either the escalation of nuclear weaponry or a policy of standing pat on the nuclear weapons already deployed. A quarter of voters consistently favoured the status quo. But a similar-sized bloc of people gave inconsistent responses, where they tended to agree with one position but also agreed with other inconsistent positions. One in twenty respondents held strongly inconsistent views, strongly agreeing or disagreeing in an inconsistent manner across the three questions. On the face of it, these findings are not very hopeful for the chances of securing majority support for non-nuclear defence policies.

But in June 1983 Labour's defence policy was based around a very undeveloped form of unilateralism, in which the alternative defence policies to be pursued after the scrapping of Trident and Polaris, and the expulsion of US

Table 5.3: The Consistency of Voters' Attitudes Towards Nuclear Weapons, LSE Election Study 1983

(Items checked for consistency are statements 2, 3 and 6 in Table 5.2).

Proportion (%) which:	Total sample	Conservat- ive voters	Alliance voters	Labour voters
Consistently favoured new nuclear weapons	37	55	29	18
Gave inconsistent responses	30	25	32	37
Consistently favoured nuclear status quo	24	19	30	24
Consistently favoured unilateral disarm- ament	9	1	9	21

Source: P. Dunleavy and C.T. Husbands, British Democracy at the Crossroads, (London, Allen and Unwin, 1985), p.178.

nuclear bases were left largely unspecified. For this reason it is fair to use the sixth item in Table 5.1 as a core index of the popularity of Labour policy at that time. However, as Mike Gapes' chapter emphasises, Labour policy presentation now stresses the strengthening of conventional defences as a consequence of ceasing to divert considerable resources into ineffective nuclear deterrence. Even in the prevailing pro-nuclear climate of the June 1983 election this shift would have had a major impact on the popular appeal of Labour policies, as Table 5.4 demonstrates.

In 1983 only a sixth of all voters, and little more than a third of even Labour voters endorsed both a policy of immediate unilateral disarmament and a refusal to allow US bases to be used for American nuclear weapons. But support for Labour's current policy position was dramatically higher, with over a third of all voters and nearly three fifths of Labour supporters consistently favouring both policies. Overall reactions for and against Labour's revised policy package were relatively evenly balanced, with a third of voters being in favour, rather over a third against, and just

Table 5.4: Voters' Attitudes in June 1983 to the Labour Party's Then Nuclear Policy and to its Contemporary (1987) Position

1983 Manifesto Policy (i.e. expulsion of US nuclear bases and unilateral disarmament come what may - disagreeing with item 4 and agreeing with item 6 in Table 5.2).

	Proportion (%) with attitudes:		
	Consistently favourable	Mixed reactions	Consistently unfavourable
Labour voters	36	41	23
Alliance voters	18	45	37
Conservative voters	2	30	68
Total sample	16	38	46

Current (1987) Policy (i.e. expulsion of US nuclear bases and defence based on strong conventional forces only - disagreeing with item 4 and agreeing with item 5 in Table 5.2).

	Proportion (%) with attitudes:		
	Consistently favourable	Mixed reactions	Consistently unfavourable
Labour voters	57	24	19
Alliance voters	36	38	27
Conservative voters	14	28	58
Total sample	34	28	38

Source: Computed from LSE Election Study data.

under 30 per cent of voters in the middle having mixed reactions. Analysing this middle group a bit further shows that in 1983 people favoured a British nuclear deterrent but those disapproving of US nuclear bases in the UK were twice as numerous as those opposed to British nuclear weapons but wishing to retain US nuclear bases here (Table 5.5).

Although the LSE study asked the most closely co-ordinated questions about different aspects of defence attitudes, its general findings are confirmed by studies with larger samples carried out subsequently. In general

5.5: Voters' Attitudes in June 1983 to Strong Conventional Defence and Retaining US Nuclear Bases

Percentages of total sample who jointly agree/disagree:

	Strong conventional defence only	
Retain US nuclear bases	Agree	Disagree
Disagree	33	18
Agree	9	37

Source: Computed from LSE Election Study data.

opposition to US nuclear bases is much stronger than Table willingness to consider nuclear disarmament for Britain, and the expression of anti-nuclear attitudes increases considerably if mention of strong conventional forces is linked with the decision to go non-nuclear.

There is not a great deal of available information on the factors which influence public opinion on nuclear defence. Pro or anti-nuclear attitudes are consistently structured by party identifications, with Labour supporters moving steadily towards greater unity behind their party's policy, a considerable minority of anti-nuclear opinions amongst supporters of the Liberal-Social Democratic Alliance, but with Conservative supporters very firmly committed to supporting both the UK nuclear deterrent and the retention of US nuclear bases. There is some strong suggestive evidence that pro- and anti-nuclear attitudes are strongly linked also with people's newspaper exposure. Whiteley demonstrates that Labour party supporters who read Conservative newspapers are particularly likely to have more fragmented attitudes than their counterparts who read Labour-inclined newspapers (Whiteley, 1985, pp.105-8). In this respect the trend in 1986 towards setting up new relatively non-partisan papers (Today and The Independent) or non-Tory titles (such as the News on Sunday and London Daily News) tended to redress the record majority of readers accounted for by Conservative-inclined newspapers in 1983-5 (Harrop, 1986). But by 1987 with the failure of the London Daily News, News on Sunday looking very fragile, and the Murdoch takeover of Today, any trend towards pluralisation of newspaper views seems to have been stifled at birth.

For the rest, pro- and anti-nuclear attitudes are

remarkably insensitive to class differences, although social class positions heavily influence most other public attitudes about policy issues in Britain. At various times women have tended to give stronger anti-nuclear responses than men on particular issues, such as sending back US cruise missiles. But a consistent gender-structured pattern of responses has not evolved, contrary to some speculation at the time when the Greenham Common camp was first set up. Anti-nuclear attitudes have been linked with a number of other non-economic issues, such as a 'liberalism/illiberalism' dimension cross-cutting the class politics of the old two-party system, or 'post-materialist' values such as ecological awareness (Whiteley, 1985). But this effect ' may be transitory, reflecting the incomplete incorporation of pro- and anti-nuclear attitudes into partisan identifications in the early 1980s. The longer the nuclear debate remains in its current form of a straight Labour/Conservative confrontation (with the Alliance occupying its customary rather confused middle ground), the more likely it is that opinion leadership influences will inhibit the linking of nuclear attitudes with issues cross-cutting party lines.

Perhaps one of the most important long-term characteristics of nuclear attitudes is the presence of a limited generational effect. Apart from the 1983 general election, people in the youngest age group (18-24 years old) have shown quite evenly balanced pro- and anti-nuclear attitudes in the 1980s, an effect which sometimes but not always extends into the 25-34 years old band. Whiteley (1985) notes that 'it is among the young that pessimism about the prospect of war is most consistent and widespread' (p.111), and argued that as generations of older voters profoundly committed to nuclear deterrence policies leave the electorate and are replaced by new voters, so the trend towards denuclearisation will gradually cumulate - whether or not many existing voters change their minds and accept non-nuclear defence policies.

IMPLEMENTING A STRATEGY FOR DENUCLEARISATION

Given the existing structure of public opinion about nuclear weapons and nuclear alliances, which is likely to change positively only in a very gradual fashion, can any general strategies enhance the probability of achieving substantive denuclearisation? In the light of the long-term prospects for

121

change I go on in the final section of the paper to examine the prospects for progress in the face of alternative political scenarios for the aftermath of the next general election in 1991-2.

Strategic thinking always confronts political parties with acute problems on issues such as nuclear disarmament. If public opinion is ever to be changed away from unbroken support for nuclear escalation then it must be offered a reasonably clear lead. Activists in the Labour party, and anti-nuclear campaigners more generally, must also be motivated to go on actively pushing for denuclearisation. But their mobilisation will typically depend upon reciprocal assurances from the Labour leadership that the party will firmly implement non-nuclear policies, without equivocation or leadership wrangles, and in the face of unmistakably hostile US and possibly European reactions. Thus unless Labour gives a clear lead on nuclear issues, the risk will be that it fails to exert any leverage (via moral example or opinion leadership) upon public opinion, and that it provides insufficient incentives to party activists and peace campaigners to sustain their continued mobilisation.

Yet the evidence of public attitudes reviewed above presents the clearest warning about the dangers of moving too far in advance of voters' views. In particular the structure of public opinion strongly suggests that voters will not easily accept any policy which appears to involve unilateral disarmament 'come what may'. Such a stance by failing to discriminate between different stages and levels of existing nuclear commitments has the effect of bundling up separable political issues into a single indigestible lump, rather than splitting denuclearisation up into bite-sized pieces which voters could begin to try out to see if they like the taste. In particular, too aggregated a first instalment of denuclearisation policies further raises the thresholds of public acceptability which must be surmounted, thereby preventing the initiation of a rolling programme altogether (see scenario 5 in the next section).

The rolling programme concept implies that Labour's current policy, even with an emphasis upon strong conventional armaments as a substitute for the dismantled nuclear arsenal, is far too ambitious as a first step. One alternative more closely in line with the rolling programme concept would have been to separate out the decisions on US nuclear bases and other nuclear weapons from the 'last ditch' decision to decommission the principal UK deterrent, whether it be the old Polaris missile submarines or part at least of the Trident programme by this stage. For example, Labour might have pledged to implement all its denuclearisation policies short of decommissioning Polaris/Trident, while negotiating an arms reduction with the Soviet Union. At the end of a previously specified period, a Labour government would bring forward proposals to dismantle Polaris/Trident for voters to decide on at a referendum (see Dunleavy and Husbands, 1984). In the event, Labour's current (1987) policies continue to emphasise the electoral indivisibility of its non-nuclear programme. But as the scenarios in the next section make clear, policy implementation in government will necessarily be a multi-stage process. And in any situation except a majority Labour administration the chances of denuclearisation being initiated at all will crucially depend upon the party's ability to deal in a discriminating fashion with different elements of its overall policy commitments.

There are a number of options currently excluded from Labour thinking which merit serious examination for inclusion in a rolling programme of denuclearisation. The referendum device is potentially useful because of its effect in separating out a single policy question for separate voter consideration. Of course, people on the left have generally suspected referenda as a device which allows the right wing leaderships of some socialist parties to renege on those major manifesto commitments which have become inconvenient. This diagnosis was certainly accurate in the 1975 British referendum on the EEC, when most of the Labour government campaigned for a 'Yes' vote after being elected on a manifesto promise to pull out of the Common Market. It also neatly fits the 1985 referendum in Spain, where the socialist government elected on a strongly anti-American platform nonetheless subsequently campaigned successfully for Spain to remain in the NATO alliance. Both these cases show how the referendum device can be used to create an apparently unified stance amongst supposedly competing party leaderships, which can command overwhelming media support and successfully isolate the anti-EEC or anti-NATO left by bringing exceptionally strong opinion leadership influences to bear on voters. Further support for such an interpretation can easily be drawn from the decision of sections of the pro-nuclear right within Labour's ranks to adopt the nuclear referendum, notably its belated advocacy by the EEPTU at the 1987 party

Conference, a stance backed by some Labour papers such as News on Sunday and Joe Haines in the Sunday People.

But it is equally true that referendum campaigns have also played a major part in achieving denuclearisation in the civil energy fields, with the 1977 Austrian vote throwing out proposals by the Social Democratic government to begin constructing the country's first nuclear plant, and the 1980 referendum in Sweden leading to a firm electoral verdict in favour of phasing out the existing nuclear energy programme within two decades. Both these last two examples also demonstrate the importance of special forms of public information and discussion channels in producing a climate of public opinion favourable for change against entrenched policy or strong established interests. The Austrian referendum followed an extended process of national scientific debate upon the advantages and dangers of nuclear power, with equal state funding and television time for both sides of the argument to be properly presented. Similarly the Swedish Social Democrats used an extensive programme of state-funded 'study circles', mostly run by the trades unions, voluntary organisations and the churches, which extensively prepared the ground for an informed public debate during their nuclear energy referendum. The important achievement in both cases was to by-pass the normal mass media-controlled and party-dominated systems of communicating political information to voters, and to create new channels where higher than normal levels of information could be communicated direct to voters who could make a more careful assessment of a single issue.

There is a final more substantive ingredient which might well have a role to play in the later stages of a denuclearisation strategy, specifically in persuading voters that the time has come to detach Britain from its membership of NATO and to switch instead towards a policy which is clearly dealigned, and possibly avowedly neutralist. Even if the current (1987) Soviet-American talks to eliminate intermediate and short-range nuclear missiles from Europe are completely successful, it is clear that this kind of issue could only arise at a very late stage in a rolling programme of denuclearisation, when the dismantling of the British nuclear missile systems and the expulsion of US nuclear bases has decisively reduced the probability of UK territory ever being involved in a direct nuclear strike. Nonetheless some prospect of a nuclear strike must remain so long as UK bases are used as listening or command posts in support of the US nuclear arsenal, given that neither Soviet nor US military decision-making could conceivably be significantly influenced or controlled by British political pressure during a nuclear crisis. Even if the UK territory was not directly exposed to nuclear strike it could still be powerfully affected by fallout from a nuclear explosion or accident anywhere in Europe. The Chernobyl power plant disaster rather forcefully raises again the question of the precautions needed to guard against a major fault in a British nuclear reactor, or indeed in the numerous French plants close to the Channel.

There is obvious scope here for the left to reconsider its traditional attitude towards civil defence. While Britain remains enmeshed in nuclear alliances held in unstable equilibrium by some version of the MAD doctrine, Labour and the left have consistently opposed civil defence. These programmes have been analysed as calculated only to mislead the public about the disastrous consequences of a nuclear exchange and to falsely assimilate nuclear arms into bogus parallels with conventional weapons - whereas, in practice, the terminology of 'winning' or 'losing' wars, or of 'defending' anything by using nuclear weapons becomes quite meaningless. Under any form of MAD situation, the enactment of effective civil defence preparations by one side or the other is also destabilising, because it calls into question the extent of the assured destruction faced by that side and its political leadership.

But once denuclearisation has proceeded to the stage where Britain no longer possesses or houses any nuclear weapons, and the critical locus of concern shifts towards separating the UK from its involvement in the NATO alliance, then these objections to an effective civil defence programme must lapse. In a non-nuclear Britain, civil defence would not destabilise a MAD balance, nor make the initiation of any form of nuclear conflict more likely. But by providing an alternative focus for security, especially in a thoroughly dealigned or even neutralist Britain, it could provide the kind of positive assurance which voters will need if they are to sever links with a nuclear alliance stretching back over 40 years. In particular a package of effective civil defence combined with strong conventional armed forces, and vigorous protection of British territorial integrity from interference by either Soviet or US military alliances, could provide the format needed to make the final stages of denuclearisation acceptable to public opinion. If similar movements were taking place elsewhere in Western and Eastern Europe at the same time, as seems perfectly conceivable by the early 1990s, then achieving sufficient momentum for such a change does not seem wildly implausible.

SCENARIOS FOR INITIATING DENUCLEARISATION IN THE SHORT-TERM

In the more immediate future, following a general election in 1991-2, or possibly two closely interspersed elections in the event of a hung Parliament, there are five possible scenarios for the chances of implementing some denuclearisation policies.

1. A majority Labour government obviously offers the greatest prospect of progress towards a non-nuclear defence policy, (leaving on one side whether such a result could realistically be achieved in a single election in 1991-2). The question marks which remain about how such a government could proceed concern the difficulties which would be placed in the path of non-nuclear initiatives by the UK defence establishment, by US policy, and by the reactions of other West European countries within NATO. The government's internal position is strengthened by the ability to implement most elements of its non-nuclear policies using executive action powers. The original funding of the nuclear deterrent and the creation of nuclear facilities were both accomplished under a mask of great secrecy. And the precise status of the operational programmes of Britain's nuclear weapons forces and facilities have always been carefully hidden from Parliamentary and mass media scrutiny. In the difficult first phases of decommissioning Polaris/Trident, it is likely that a Labour government will want to preserve much of this traditional insulation. In addition the arrangements for US military bases which have been agreed since 1945 were all set up in a highly deformalised manner. They will require to be closely renegotiated with the US government, but not to be reviewed or approved in detail by Parliament. Consequently a Labour government should be able to dismantle nuclear weapons facilities and appropriations

without detailed legislative scrutiny, and to rearrange the terms on which bases are afforded to the Americans under the mantle of Crown prerogative powers. There is relatively little scope therefore for government actions to be obstructed by defections of isolated Labour MPs on particular Commons votes or by opposition in the House of Lords.

Hence the crucial locus of opposition of Labour policies will probably lie within the Ministry of Defence and the armed forces themselves. So long as Polaris remains operational service opposition to the scrapping of Trident contracts may be relatively constrained, since the interests of the RAF and the Army might be capable of being mobilised against the certain strong opposition of the Navy. The Labour Shadow Cabinet's considerations of implementation-resistance have certainly relied heavily on the feasibility of 'divide and rule' strategies for overcoming the Services' opposition. But much more concerted objections are likely to become manifest once Trident actually forms the operational deterrent, not least because of the substantial contract penalties involved in cancelling the programme once it is well advanced. Similar controversy is certain to envelop the severing of nuclear links which the withdrawal of US missiles, bombers, and other nuclear delivery systems would entail. The substantial intelligence and weapons system information exchanges which currently occur would be jeopardised, and a degree of dislocation in some NATO command systems would be entailed by these Labour commitments.

The prospect of a co-ordinated internal resistance to the implementation of non-nuclear policies would increase severely if the Labour government was elected on a relatively low proportion of the total votes polled (in the range between 39 and 43 per cent) which seems the only feasible possibility of any Labour majority. If service chiefs could see good prospects of the demise of the Labour administration within a year or two of its gaining control, then internal obstruction of policy on US nuclear bases, Polaris decommissioning and Trident cancellation would be near-certain. The tough policy already signalled by the USA during 1986-7 in the run-up to the last election strongly suggests that such internal opposition would be powerfully fuelled by the threat of US resources being diverted away from NATO, perhaps in the politically sensitive form of troop withdrawals. Finally objections from West Germany,

Italy and the Benelux countries against the expulsion of US nuclear bases could intensify these difficulties.

All these considerations suggest that a carefully organised rolling programme would still be essential if a Labour government was to achieve denuclearisation which was sustainable. While cancelled Trident contracts might never be fully renewed, there is every prospect that a Conservative government elected within five years of a Labour victory could simply reinvite the USA to utilise UK bomber bases for nuclear strike purposes, could resuscitate Polaris or partially completed Trident submarines unless they had physically been broken up in the meantime, and could even consider devices such as a cruise-armed submarine force. Nor will the scientific capacity for manufacturing British nuclear warheads have disappeared, since it will continue to be necessary throughout the period of Polaris decommissioning. The difficult questions for a majority Labour government do not therefore concern its administrative competence or the strength of its political will in an almost certainly hostile political climate. Its crucial task is instead to take those steps towards denuclearisation which are feasible in such a way as to create a self-sustaining transformation of public opinion, which alone can guarantee that non-nuclear policies are entrenched as irreversible features of the British political landscape.

2.   A minority Labour government would clearly be considerably impeded by its lack of a legislative majority. But the considerations about executive action outlined in the first scenario mean that its freedom of action would still remain considerable. The exercise of Crown prerogative powers and ministerial decisions on regulations, treaties and foreign agreements does not require that ministers consult with Parliamentarians outside the government's own ranks. Of course, if ministers in a minority government embark on a course of action which a majority of the Commons disapprove of, then they are liable to be faced by motions of censure against the government or of no confidence in the individually responsible minister.

Inherently, censure motions cannot be used except on large issues, and if a Labour minority government survives at all it is presumably because it offers concessions to minority parties (such as Scottish Nationalist, Plaid Cymru and SDLP MPs) in return for being sustained in office. Conceivably a minority Labour administration might be able to secure limited legislative agreements with the Alliance (on the lines of the 1977 Lib-Lab pact). Although such a deal would almost certainly not cover key defence issues, its existence could still usefully insulate a Labour administration in its use of executive action powers. Thus unless such deals had collapsed anyway, a minority government could probably 'tough out' censure motions. As for no-confidence motions in individual ministers, it really remains quite obscure how effective they could be as a post-hoc constraint on the use of executive action powers by ministers in a minority administration. They were not an important constraint during the 1976-9 Labour government.

However, both censure motions on the government as a whole, and attempts to unseat individual ministers over nuclear policy, might well become much more threatening if they link up with a substantial degree of defence establishment opposition to government policy initiatives. For example, one contingency plan discussed by Ministry of Defence and military officials in 1981 (when Labour first adopted its non-nuclear policies) involved the simultaneous resignation of all the defence Chiefs of Staff and a service-wide boycott of their posts (Dunleavy and Husbands, 1984, pp.11-12). It is significant in this respect that recently retired service chiefs intervened during the 1987 general election campaign to condemn Labour's policies and apparently to call publicly for resistance to them by current service chiefs should Labour be elected. When Mrs Thatcher was asked on television about the chiefs of staff resigning rather than agreeing to implement Labour policies, she went out of her way to legitimate the idea. So there is every reason to expect that any development of this kind would very quickly become intensely threatening for a minority Labour government, making the management of dissent inside the government-military machine a high priority for the government's survival.

The other main limitation on a minority Labour government would be its inability to plan for a full Commons term, and the considerable likelihood that its implementation of denuclearisation policies would be abruptly cut short by another election, probably not precipitated by the government itself. Hence a premium would have to be placed on promoting whatever non-reversible elements of a denuclearisation policy could be implemented in a short timescale. Given the continuation of current trends towards the denuclearisation of Europe, it is conceivable that renegotiation of the US military presence could also be pushed ahead within a 2 or 3 year period. Similarly it would be relatively easy to initiate disarmament talks with the Soviet Union and to seek to alter NATO's strategy on the first-use of nuclear weapons. A sustained programme of public debate and education about nuclear weapons issues could also be set in train, swinging the full weight of the government machine behind expanding public opinion support for denuclearisation. Even the de-commissioning of Polaris and scrapping of Trident might still just be achievable depending on: (a) the stage which the Trident programme had reached and the penalties attaching to cancellation; (b) a full consultation period; (c) a period of debate about the level and type of defence commitments Britain could afford in the probably straitened economic circumstances of the 1990s; and (d) a degree of support from some Alliance MPs. But the timescale here would seem to stretch over a much longer period than a minority government would be able (or would want) to maintain itself in office.

3.   A Labour/Alliance coalition government may still seem unlikely, but such a hybrid administration could result if both parties make real moves toward convergence before the next election, or if two successive general elections produce hung Parliaments. Because executive action and public campaign powers (plus, of course, all new legislation) would have to be agreed between both partners, a coalition government including Labour ministers would be very much worse for the prospects of achieving denuclearisation than a minority Labour administration. Nuclear defence issues would no longer be bundled up within the overall fabric of governmental policy for the purposes of inter-party dealings or Parliamentary scrutiny. Instead Labour leaders would have to negotiate each stage of denuclearisation directly with Alliance ministers.

So the likelihood is that progress would be strictly limited to (at best) the freezing of investments in British nuclear capabilities, partial withdrawal from the full implementation of the Trident programme, and the initiation of negotiations with the USA about nuclear bases. A mixed Polaris/Trident nuclear deterrent force would undoubtedly survive such an administration, and even the removal of US nuclear bases would be problematic. The only discernible compensating advantage is that voters might find the scrapping of part of the Trident contracts less threatening if brought forward by a coalition government, making it easier to enact immediately than under a minority Labour administration. The Alliance's direct involvement in government decision-making might also be expected to reignite the divisions over nuclear issues demonstrated by the Liberal Assembly's 1986 rejection of the joint Alliance leadership's defence policy document. Both the Liberals and Social Democrats have been leader-dominated parties until now, with such a drastic shortage of elected MPs that party in-fighting has been artificially suppressed (Drucker and Gamble, 1986). Hence it is not inconceivable that exposure to real ministerial power could trigger the rapid growth of distinctive factions, with quite a strong Liberal anti-nuclear campaign as one of the most important of these groupings. But by the same token the recently-sublimated divisions over nuclear policy inside the Labour leadership are likely to re-emerge rather forcefully within any sort of coalition government.

4.   A Conservative/Alliance coalition government is highly unlikely to initiate any substantial steps towards denuclearisation, but compared with a Conservative government with an outright Commons majority it might still have some positive impact in preventing or delaying the full escalation of Britain's nuclear capability which is currently government policy. The most which could be hoped for is that the Trident contract remained outside the general framework of Tory/Alliance collaboration, and could therefore be somewhat reduced by a Parliamentary vote uniting Labour and Alliance MPs. But the more probable outcome is that such a large step could not remain outside the inter-party deal. Hence we could expect to see a re-evaluation or longer phasing-in of the Trident contract, or a reduction in the degree of escalation which it will entail (e.g. by not filling all the available missile tubes in the Trident submarines). Conceivably the suppressed debate within the Tories' ranks about the type of defence capabilities which it is feasible for Britain to maintain could be re-opened by decisions along these lines, especially since less expensive forms of nuclear deterrence (such as

submarine-launched cruise missiles) might be reconsidered. But it is equally likely that at the end of a re-evaluation process Alliance MPs could be swayed into accepting the existing contracts as a fait accompli.

5.   A fourth majority Conservative government will very considerably set back the longer-term chances of achieving denuclearisation by pressing ahead with the full implementation of the Trident programme. There is a well-recognised general tendency for public opinion to accept the status quo in government policy, and a case could be made out for this tendency being strongly established in majority attitudes to defence issues. When Trident submarines are built and the Polaris deterrent is decommissioned, then the British nuclear deterrent protected by pro-nuclear public opinion majorities will be a qualitatively more threatening and powerful system than has been the case hitherto. The weapons system's life-span will also tend to postpone any policy reappraisal (whereas Polaris' declining effectiveness has opened up the nuclear debate during the 1980s). In short a considerable window of opportunity will have been closed.

CONCLUSION

Public opinion surveys are inherently static: they tell us what voters' existing attitudes may be, but not how, how much, or why they will change. Such dynamic questions remain as open areas for the exercise of political judgement, especially the judgement of those politicians who by controlling the state apparatus acquire a considerably enhanced capacity to shape the evolution of public opinion. I have argued here that the most fundamental change of viewpoint needed from advocates of denuclearisation in the Labour party and outside is a recognition of the need for strategic thinking in pushing ahead changes in defence policies which can endure and be self-sustaining in public opinion terms. Conceiving of denuclearisation as a rolling programme recognises contradictory imperatives - on the one hand, to stay in touch with public opinion so as to secure the opportunities to begin implementing non-nuclear defence policies; but on the other hand, to continuously push back the frontiers of public acceptability and to (eventually) lead voters to reappraise Britain's current position within the NATO military alliance.

REFERENCES

Crewe, I. (1987), 'Tories prosper from a paradox', The Guardian, 16 June, p.4

Drucker, H. and Gamble, A. (1986) 'The party system', in H. Drucker, P. Dunleavy, A. Gamble and G. Peele (eds), Developments in British Politics, (London: Macmillan), pp.60-86

Dunleavy, P. and Husbands, C.T. (1984), 'One last chance: the case for a nuclear referendum', New Socialist, no. 19, November, pp.7-12

Dunleavy, P. and Husbands, C.T. (1985), British Democracy at the Crossroads: Voting and Party Competition in the 1980s, (London: Allen and Unwin)

Dunleavy, P. and Ward, H. (1981) 'Exogenous voter preferences and parties with state power: some internal problems of economic theories of party competition', British Journal of Political Science, vol. 11, no. 3, pp.351-80

Harrop, M. (1986), 'The press and post-war elections', in I. Crewe and M. Harrop (eds), Political Communications: The 1983 General Election Campaign (Cambridge: Cambridge University Press), pp.137-49

Whiteley, P. (1985), 'Attitudes to defence and international affairs', in R. Jowell and S. Witherspoon (eds) British Social Attitudes 1985 (Farnborough, Hants: Gower), pp.95-119

Chapter Six

A STRATEGIC CONCLUSION

Gordon Burt

In the introduction to this book I argued that British defence policy is in crisis. The crisis is partly a reflection of radical changes in the distribution of world power and partly a reflection of the fact that nuclear weapons introduce a qualitatively new factor into military speculations. The crisis is particularly acute for Britain in view of its dramatic post-war decline as a military, economic and imperial power. Major flaws can be found in our defence policy at all levels: at the level of the superpower confrontation itself, at the level of NATO strategy, at the level of Britain's role in NATO and even at the level of British domestic politics.

In view of the crisis, in view of these flaws, it is not surprising that challenges to existing policy are becoming more frequent and more radical, both in Britain and in the world as a whole. Our aim in this book has been to move beyond criticisms of the existing policy and onto the consideration of an alternative policy and its implementation. In Chapter 2, Andrew Kelly has argued that present NATO strategy is dangerous and unnecessary. For it involves the questionable assumption that conventional defences would be over-run in any Warsaw Pact attack. On the basis of his analysis of the existing and potential military dispositions, Kelly has pointed the way to an alternative strategy based on strengthening the conventional deterrent. In contrast with these proposals there has been recent discussion in NATO of conventional strategies in Europe in the context of the existing nuclear balance. In Chapter 3, Philip Gummett has considered these NATO strategies and has noted that they present an increased danger of escalation, and has cast doubt on some of the optimistic claims which have been made about the 'new technology'. Broadening out from this focus on the military dimension, the following chapter by Mike Gapes has charted the course of Labour's defence policy from its disarray in the 1983 election to its more coherent formulation in the 1987 election. An obvious pre-requisite for the implementation of a non-nuclear defence policy is that a Labour government be elected. Here, two alternative strategies present themselves. Whereas Gapes would advocate presenting the electorate with a clear commitment to implement an alternative defence policy, Patrick Dunleavy has proposed a rolling programme whereby components of a non-nuclear policy are introduced stage by stage in step with a progressively developing public opinion. An analysis of public opinion data has shown us which policy components might be implemented now and which ones require further debate. Dunleavy has indicated what this stage-by-stage approach might look like in the context of five different electoral scenarios.

What I would like to do now in this final chapter is to step back from the arguments in the previous chapters and, as it were, to view them from the outside. First I would like to consider both the viewpoints in this book and also alternative viewpoints in the light of the conceptual requirements of any defence policy. Then I would like to consider the location in society of this debate between viewpoints, by examining the politics of the debate. This will raise certain questions about what is going on (or should be going on) in the conduct of this debate. We shall discover that the debate - and hence the move towards alternative defence - is severely restricted by the concentration of power in the establishment. This means that alternative defence policy may require in part a struggle for real democracy. However, to recognise this as a goal is not enough: there is a need to develop an appropriate political strategy.

(Note: I shall be using the concepts of 'the establishment' and 'real democracy' quite extensively in what follows. So it is worthwhile spelling out in greater detail what I mean by them. The notion of 'the establishment' involves an assertion that certain individuals or groups or organisations occupy a certain (possibly formal) role in society as a result of which they exert a greater amount of power than other individuals, groups or organisations. Clearly there is some ambiguity in this concept. How much excess power ... how formal a role ... is required to qualify one for membership of the establishment? However this does not matter too much as most of the statements I shall be making about the establishment apply whether a narrow or a broad interpretation is used. Moreover I see my claims as representing tendencies rather than universal truths: some parts of the establishment and some parts of the non-establishment will deviate from their respective norms. In this way I can accommodate for the fact that the establishment is not monolithic but is fractured in various ways. For example different fractions of the establishment can be found in the civil service, in the parties, in industry, in the media and in the academic world. With our focus on defence we are particularly interested in the Ministry of Defence, party defence spokespersons, the defence industry, the military, and media reporters and academics with a defence orientation. An alternative defence policy 'will be confronting not a single powerful and permanent establishment, but a dozen establishments strongly opposed to some aspects of its policy.' (1)

It is such opposition that raises fundamental problems for what we have grown accustomed to call 'democracy'. What price voting, if the establishment rules? Thus what we call 'democracy' today is characterised by inequality of power. This may or may not be a good system of government (!), but it scarcely counts as rule by the people. 'Real democracy' - real rule by the people - would involve equality of power. When or whether absolute equality of power can be achieved is a matter for debate. What is clear is that there are many steps which can be taken to reduce inequality of power. Because this inequality of power in part depends on the establishment's occupation of key roles in society, an important step would be to secure democratic appointment to these roles. Furthermore these democratic procedures would need to be such as to ensure a fair representation of disadvantaged groups in society whether the disadvantage arises through class, gender, race or regional relations.)

WHAT SHOULD DEFENCE POLICY BE?

Let us start then by considering the alternatives to alternative defence! On the one hand there are those who, while acknowledging the value of the various proposals in this book, might wish to argue that our focus on the East-West confrontation had failed to acknowledge the underlying primacy of some other issue. Variously they might argue that the North-South confrontation, or class relations or patriarchy was the determining factor, and that the East-West confrontation could not be resolved without addressing this prime factor. On the other hand there are those who, while not disagreeing with a desire to reduce East-West tension, might feel that there was an imbalance in any proposal which demanded progress on the military front in advance of progress on the political front. They would want to see much greater progress towards political detente before taking any significant steps towards alternative defence. Finally, there are those who are not unhappy about nuclear weapons: such weapons have kept the peace for forty years, it will be alright with Star Wars, we will win the economic war, we will win the nuclear war, and Armageddon is promised in the Bible.

In order to provide a framework for comparing these viewpoints, it is worthwhile reflecting further on the nature of the problem. What is conceptually required by the question: 'What should British defence policy be?' Clearly, in order to answer this, we need an adequate conception of policy prescription and an adequate conception of defence. Moreover the term 'should' is critical. It points to the fact that we need to make judgments about competing policies, that these judgments need to be made in terms of certain criteria, and that these criteria need to be justified by some rationale deriving from a theory of values. Also, Britain does not exist in isolation from the rest of the world. Nor is the defence sphere isolated from the rest of society. So any consideration of defence must be embedded in a consideration of world society as a whole. All these components interact: interactions between theory and perceptual experience, interactions between theory and values, and interactions between conceptions of world society and of defence.

The purpose of spelling all this out is to reveal the reasons why evaluation of the defence debate is so difficult. The diagram reveals to us the vast theoretical underpinning

Figure 6.1: The conceptual requirements for a defence policy

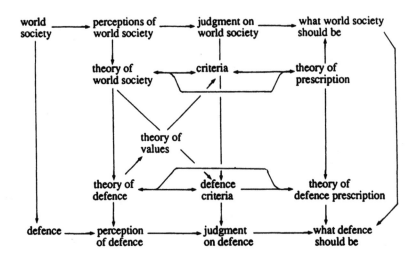

which most assertions about defence have. Any debate about a defence statement must involve not only a restricted debate on the specific military situation under examination, but it must also raise broader questions about each of the aspects discussed above. (Of course, I am not quite correct in saying 'must involve'. The debates, by mutual consent or by unilateral imposition, may choose to make certain assumptions and to take these for granted.) The existence of these broader considerations is illustrated on the one hand by the early arguments for the UK's possession of the bomb in terms of guaranteeing 'our seat at the top table', and on the other hand by the peace movement's rejection of nuclear weapons on moral grounds.

We shall now discuss the competing views in terms of this framework - with the appreciation that the debate is not just between different military theorems, but it is also between different ways of looking at the world. First there are disagreements about who or what are the significant actors or forces or relationships in the world. Are world events primarily about relations between states or are they about relations between classes ... or even about relations between the sexes? Is history determined by military power, or by technology, or by economics, or by ...?

It might seem that these broad abstract questions are far removed from our concern with British defence policy. Yet if we ever do manage to get rid of nuclear weapons from British soil it will be due in no small measure to the women at Greenham, and to the world view which has guided their actions - a world view which sees patriarchy as a major determinant of society and, in particular, as an important determinant of nuclear defence policy. (2)

An alternative world view sees global class relations as being the central characteristic of the world today. 'Bread, not bombs!'. Thus there is considerable support - even from the establishment - for the idea that the East-West confrontation exacerbates the problems faced by the peoples of the Third World. (3) Other analysts go further and argue that the East-West confrontation is a convenient strategy toward the more basic goal of stabilising the unequal relations between North and South. (4)

Moreover a similar argument is applied to domestic politics: the East-West confrontation is seen as a useful device for internal control: the 'enemy within' is discredited because they are the 'agents' of the 'enemy without'.

In the discussion of military matters, a different focus is more usual. Here <u>states</u> are regarded as the significant actors. And in the main this is the viewpoint adopted in most of the chapters in this book. Historically people have mobilised round national banners rather than class or gender ones. People, blissfully uncaring about torture under the Argentinian dictatorship, were happy to indulge in the jingoism of the Falklands/Malvinas dispute. Happy or not, in services or in civvies, we are all conscripts of the national security state. (5) If we define the nation-state as that political entity which has the monopoly over the legitimate use of violence, then a focus on military questions would seem to lead naturally to a focus on states. In this view, world affairs are constituted by the struggle between states, a struggle in many spheres, with military action offering the ultimate recourse.

Thus we find starkly different views of the world ...

characterised by relations between states, with a focus on the military sphere ... by relations between classes with a focus on the economic sphere ... or by relations between the sexes with a focus on the social sphere. How are we to assess these? Firstly it seems clear that all these aspects exist. Also, in some situations state relations will be the dominant dimension while in other situations class or gender relations may be dominant. Moreover these dimensions interact in complex ways. For this reason I find it difficult to accept claims that any one dimension has primacy. In saying this I am making an important distinction between significance and power. Particularly in military situations the power of states is very evident: in an important sense the arms race is powerfully determined by the relations between the superpower states. However, equally clear is the significance of class relations and gender relations in moderating this situation. What this means is that our theory of world society needs to involve an interplay between these dimensions.

However the debate is not just about who or what has power in world society. It is also about who is good and who is bad ... about what constitutes good and what constitutes bad. For the participants in the debate possess markedly different values and different moralities. For example, the basic morality which seems to guide Thatcherite foreign and defence policy is essentially a capitalist and militarist one as illustrated by such diverse events as its willing compromises with apartheid in South Africa, and its acceptance of the US use of UK bases in the bombing raid on Libya. For many of us the 'morality' of Thatcherism has to be rejected because it fails to recognise the importance of justice and equality. In addition to this, the 'morality' can be rejected on intellectual grounds: it is much too simplistic to be consistent with the complexity of events in the real world.

At the moment in the UK much of Tory and Alliance politics is concerned with distancing itself from the abrasive Thatcherite morality. Certainly this involves less provocative utterances and gives the impression of somewhat greater intellectual sophistication. But as before we find the same acceptance of exploitation, and the same lack of even-handedness. For example, in his note of dissent to the Report of the Joint SDP-Liberal Alliance Commission on Defence and Disarmament, we find Brian May rejecting this 'morality' with the following words:

Taking into account the predominant Western influence in many Third World countries, which is largely a legacy of imperialism, and the continued exploitation and cultural dislocation of Afro-Asian societies by the Western civilisation, I cannot accept the report's perception that the Soviet Union is expansionist while the West is only engaged in mutually beneficial co-operation. (6)

The deficiencies in these moralities have important consequences for defence policies. Firstly, the acceptance of greed, inequality and injustice seems to be associated with the acceptance of war as just another form of competition - the survival of the fittest. Secondly, the lack of even-handedness leads to an over-estimation of the worth of oneself and one's country and an underestimation of the 'enemy'. This encourages an aggressive posture towards the enemy - which leads to an escalation of hostility. In this way the morality provides a rationale for the adoption of an aggressive defence policy and for the formation of the national security state.

Instead what is needed is a morality which recognises the complexity of the real world and which asserts the importance of peace and justice.

Let us now turn to the more narrowly-conceived defence aspects of the problem. Here the two main dimensions would appear to be the perceived danger of the present situation and the willingness to do something about it. A consideration of the various viewpoints suggests that these two dimensions are related. The establishment viewpoint possesses a charming mystical complacency: 'We might have arrived where we are for many of the wrong reasons, but the current position has a powerful rationale.' 'Major changes would seriously disrupt the delicate compromises and balances contained within the existing posture.' 'British defence policy would seem to have a degree of subtlety that is not always fully appreciated by critics.' (7)

We did not expect to reach new, specific and agreed solutions to the policy and resources dilemmas which face our defence planners ... our discussion again and again highlighted the practical constraints which are imposed upon any significant change in British defence policy by the realities of international political relationships. (8)

As in the last quotation even where there is some (limited) admission of a problem, one often finds extreme reluctance to do anything about it. Various stalling tactics are used. 'Yes, but not now!' and 'Not until ...' are frequently heard. On a first hearing the 'Let's solve the political problems before we move on defence' argument appears most reasonable. The defect in this kind of argument is that the linkage between the political and the military situations is two-way. One might just as well argue 'Let's move on defence first, before trying to tackle the political problems.' However the fundamental defect in the establishment viewpoint shows up in their determination not to address the political problem, or indeed in their willingness to exacerbate it. This is the point made by Brian May's concluding remark in his note of dissent: 'Finally, although the attitudes of some of the commission have been moderated, statements remain that will be unnecessarily offensive to the Soviet Union and are inconsistent with the expressed desire for better relations with it.' (9)

It might be suggested that I have been rather unfair on the establishment. I have described their viewpoint as possessing 'a charming mystical complacency', but what exactly is wrong with the statements quoted above? Well, they all have a distinct 'Yes Minister' flavour! They are all extremely effective as debate-stoppers and as defences of the status quo. Yes, there are obstacles to change (as discussed by the authors of this book). But that is quite different from devoting all one's energies to making sure that change does not happen.

SITUATING THE DEFENCE DEBATE IN SOCIETY

We now need to situate this debate in society. Which actors in world society are taking which positions in the debate? To a first approximation, it is a debate between those who have power in world society and those who have not: those with power are in favour of the nuclear status quo. We can observe this at all levels: as when the representatives of the South complain that the confrontation between the superpowers is a dangerous distortion of the global agenda; as when neutral countries in the North such as Finland and Sweden and Yugoslavia consistently adopt positions in international fora against the arms race; as when weaker members of the blocs (e.g. Spain, New Zealand, Denmark and Romania) dissociate in varying degrees from the central tenets of their respective alliances; as when dissident and suppressed groups (CND in the UK, and the dissident peace groups in Eastern Europe) adopt radical critiques of their own government's involvement in the arms race; as when parties (such as the Labour Party) representing the poorer and weaker sections of society challenge the nuclear priorities of parties (such as the Tory/Alliance parties) representing the establishment; as when weaker rank-and-file sections of parties challenge the nuclear priorities of their establishment-oriented leadership - as illustrated in the history of the Labour party, and in the Liberal party's conference debacle for David Steel in 1986; as when minority religions (such as the Quakers) challenge the establishment religion's passing by the nuclear issue on the other side; as when the ecology movement on a budget of thousands of pounds seeks to advertise in reply to the nuclear industry's million-pound publicity - only to have its advertisement suppressed; as when peace studies are fragilely supported on slender budgets while war studies 'blossom' with government money; (10) as when the questioning approach of peace studies in schools is libelled as propaganda, while sexism, racism and the glorification of war and authoritarianism go unchallenged in certain school locations; as when the peace movement supports itself with unpaid or low-wage labour while the military-industrial complex has the economic power to exploit a large percentage of the world's labour power; as when science and technology for humanity is starved of funds or distorted by the diversion of scientific and technological resources to military purposes in general and to nuclear purposes in particular.

To repeat, the debate is between those who have power in world society and those who have not. This is so, whichever location, whichever sphere, of society we examine. The advocates of nuclear strategy are in control of the dominant regions and the dominant states of the world, they are in control of the dominant economic forces, they are in control of the dominant cultural forces and they are in control of the dominant ideological forces.

This hegemonic power has consequences. Hegemonic power is used to perpetuate itself. The media and the educational system are used to ensure that, in many people's minds, there is no alternative. Selective recruitment for key positions takes place to ensure that questioning minds are rejected, and when selection policy proves faulty active suppression of questioning minds takes place (e.g. the persecution of certain scientists in the nuclear industry, government pressure on leaders of the peace movement, the repression against trade unionists at GCHQ Cheltenham, etc).

Of course this hegemonic power is fragmented. Clearly the two superpowers exercise a dual hegemony and are locked in mutual struggle. Also the European partners in NATO are critical of the United States. However perhaps the most distracting dimension of fragmentation is that between the self-styled 'rational' establishment and what might be labelled as the 'ideological' establishment. This distinction is enshrined in the international relations literature: there the world is characterised by power politics ... it is considered best for national leaders to play the power game, taking decisions based on rational calculations involving a realistic assessment of the power structure and of the national interest ... one of the greatest dangers to this scheme is the existence of national leaders with ideological zeal ... for their ideology clouds their judgment, they are unable to make rational calculations and realistic assessments, and so they fail to act in their own (nation's) self-interest - to the detriment of all. For long the West has viewed itself as the 'rational' actor in world politics, and has seen the Soviet Union as dangerous, not just because of its military strength but because of its 'ideological' commitment. This has been a matter of debate in the West with some people arguing for policies based on the assumption that the Soviet Union acts on a 'rational' basis, while others argued for policies based on the assumption that it acts on an 'ideological' basis. (11) The advent of Thatcher and Reagan (i.e. the coming to power of the sub-culture they represent) has reversed the argument. Certain sections of the establishment fear that Thatcher and Reagan are not 'rational' actors in the above sense. For these two leaders are quite open about their ideological commitment. It follows that these leaders are a danger to global stability. And so we find significant sectors of the ('rational') establishment seeking a safer way of preserving their hegemony. In the UK this reveals itself in the emerging regrouping in the Tory party around wet-toryism, and also in the ('rational') establishment control of the dominant positions in the Alliance parties. Just one illustration of this is the Alliance report 'Defence and Disarmament ...' with the Chairman's prefatory commitment to the continuation of Britain as a nuclear weapon state ... and the peripheralisation of Brian May to a token note of dissent. (12)

Without wishing to identify myself with Thatcher and Reagan's ideological commitment (!) it is important that we stop to consider the major defects in the 'rational' power politics view possessed by the 'rational' establishment. The most severe conceptual flaw is its denial of ideology. ('You have an ideology. I have reason.') At a stroke this move pre-empts any serious consideration on an equal basis of competing views. From a practical point of view it tends to generate recommendations which tend to preserve the existing power structure. Far from being a neutral, dispassionate, rational objective analysis of the world, the theory of power is itself an ideology. The division of Europe - and all that that implies - is a monument to this ideology of power politics.

This ideology is reproduced by an intellectual establishment consisting of a network of people drawn from the government, the military, industry and academia. The network is powerful and well-resourced. It either attracts or selects persons adhering to the establishment viewpoint. In many ways it is a closed community cut off from the rest of society - particularly from dissentient voices - and hence it tends to be a victim of 'groupthink'. It selectively advises other power locations in society. And, importantly, it provides the 'experts' giving 'informed opinion' to the media.

Of course debates between viewpoints do take place. However it is important to appreciate the politics of such debates. Firstly, participation is biased in favour of establishment viewpoints. Secondly, establishment participants (naturally) set an establishment agenda within an establishment conceptual framework, with studious neglect of non-establishment ideas.

A CALL TO DEMOCRACY

Our focus on the politics of the debate has brought to our attention the undemocratic concentration of power in the establishment. But there is still another deviation from democracy - if we take democracy to involve the freedom to achieve one's full potential in moral and intellectual development. For self-interest leads the establishment to be entrapped by their own ideology. Also the power of the establishment is used to entrap others in an alien ideology. This entrapment in a limited ideology is a powerful constraint against development of one's own full potential. To remedy this we need to construct the debate so that the purpose is not to win, but to facilitate emancipation from restricted viewpoints. Each person needs to realise that their ideology is mightily determined by their location in society and by their exposure to power in society. There is consequently a need to seek development by exploring other locations and by seeking the counter-balancing views of the weaker forces in society. This leads me to the notion that participation provides an opportunity for **development**: development of one's own views ... and facilitation of the development of others' views; development in the sense of greater sophistication ... and development in the sense of a fundamental transformation of viewpoints.

We are often told by the establishment that nuclear weapons are essential to the defence of democracy. Nothing could be further from the truth. Nuclear weapons provide a pretext for curtailing democracy: 'You cannot have open government, because that would endanger our security'. Also, just as nuclear weapons are a deterrent against democracy, so lack of democracy ensures the retention of nuclear weapons: the establishment rules, and the establishment rules that we retain nuclear weapons.

Therefore it is not surprising that the campaign to get rid of nuclear weapons becomes associated with the broader campaign for greater democracy: for the democratic accountability of government to parliament, for the democratic accountability of M.I.5, for democratic (as opposed to capitalist) control of the media, for democratic entry and progression through the civil service, for democratic control over business, for democratic entry and progression through academia and for resistance to powerful foreign constraints on and interference in our democratic processes.

POLITICAL STRATEGY

So far in this chapter the argument has been that an alternative defence policy is a desirable goal, and that

146

concentrations of power in society are obstacles to reaching this goal. What is required in the next part of the argument is clear. One needs to discover a path which will lead to the desired goal. One needs to formulate a political strategy.

It is fairly clear that if one wants to implement an alternative defence policy, one needs to secure a Labour government. On the basis of this assumption, Patrick Dunleavy and Mike Gapes consider alternative strategies for handling the defence issue. In addition to this, there is the broader question of which political strategies would secure a Labour government. In a sense, the handling of the defence issue is the least of Labour's problems!

Following the 1987 General Election - and even before it - there have been a plethora of analyses and recommendations concerning the Conservative's grip on power and what the appropriate strategic response should be. People from all parties have joined in the debate. (13)

Part of the debate focuses on arguments concerning overall trends in party support: the rise of the third party vote, and the decline of the Labour party vote from its 1945-70 levels. Associated with this are analyses of changing patterns in the structure of society, with fewer voters belonging to sectors of society which have traditionally voted Labour. This has led some to argue that Labour might need to rethink its policies - or at least the strategy for their implementation. This has been argued in particular with respect to defence - as illustrated in this volume by the debate between Gapes and Dunleavy. In contrast to this focus on policy matters, it has been suggested that the Conservatives won in 1987 through superior manipulation of images, ideas and ideologies. Labour's commitment to traditionalism was unable to construct a majority. For the future it needs to have 'an alternative scenario to Thatcherism ... a strategy for modernisation and an image of modernity.' (14)

Whatever view we take on these debates, it is clear that party political prospects in general are highly relevant to the more specific concerns of this book. This illustrates the extent to which considerations of defence policy impinge on a variety of social issues. In this chapter we have seen how defence policy depends on the kind of society one values ... how concentrations of power in society obstruct the development of more rational defence policies ... how political strategies need to be developed for the implementation of these policies ... how political strategies

147

shade into cultural strategies.

This is reflected in the sequencing of the arguments in this book, starting with a specific focus on defence policy per se in the chapters by Andrew Kelly and Philip Gummett, and then moving onto the broader political questions examined by Mike Gapes and Patrick Dunleavy. In this way the book conveys two broad messages. First that there are sound reasons for seeking a fundamental change to existing defence policy. Second that effective political strategies need to be developed for bringing about that change of policy as soon as possible.

NOTES AND REFERENCES

1.   Oxford Research Group. Who decides? An ORG study of British nuclear weapon decision-making, 1986.
2.   Reardon, B.A., Sexism and the war system. Teachers College Press, 1985.
3.   'In confronting the great economic and social problems of the Third World, we recognise that the trade in armaments can contribute to economic decline' (p.10). 'Our proposals for arms control, disarmament and disengagement ... are designed ... also to release resources for world development.' (p.1). Defence and Disarmament. Report of the Joint SDP-Liberal Alliance Commission. Hebden Royd on behalf of the Liberal-SDP Alliance, 1986.
4.   'The linkage between local (Third World) and global (great power) militarisation is made and sustained through arms trade and training ... For the superpowers, geopolitical considerations predominate. The transfer of weapons and training is regarded as a means of sustaining dominant/dependent relations and continuing hegemonic rivalry.' Kim, S.S. The Quest for a Just World Order, Westview, 1984.
5.   Yergin, D. Shattered Peace. The origins of the Cold War and the National Security State, Deutsch, 1977.
6.   See Brian May's Note of Dissent, in Defence and Disarmament, (op.cit.).
7.   Williams, P. Meeting Alliance and National Needs, in Roper, J. (ed.), The Future of British Defence Policy, Gower, 1985, p.10.
8.   Admiral Sir James Eberle. Foreward to Roper (op.cit.).
9.   Brian May, (op.cit.).

10. Of course the number of Ministry of Defence lectureships in war studies departments is not great - although rather more than the number of government-funded lectureships in peace studies! The real dramatic disparity arises as soon as we count in the implicit war studies which goes on in universities, in the defence industry and in government itself. For example the Royal United Services Institute has a regular bulletin in this field. Also, not infrequently academic seminars in this area include participants from the defence industry.

11. Shenfield, S. The nuclear predicament: explorations in Soviet ideology. Chatham House Paper No.37, Royal Institute of International Affairs, 1987.

12. Defence and Disarmament, (op.cit.).

13. Analyses, predictions and prescriptions have appeared regularly during June in the Guardian. Fuller articles have appeared in Marxism Today, New Socialist and New Statesman both prior to and after the election.

14. Hall, S. Blue election, election blues. Marxism Today, 30-35, July 1987.

INDEX

For Product Safety Concerns and Information please contact our EU
representative GPSR@taylorandfrancis.com
Taylor & Francis Verlag GmbH, Kaufingerstraße 24, 80331 München, Germany